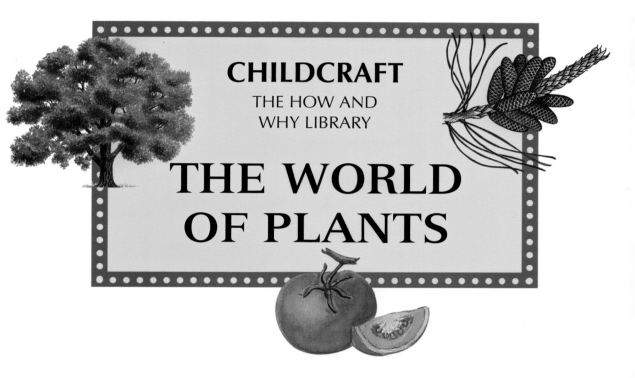

# CHILDCRAFT
### THE HOW AND
### WHY LIBRARY

# THE WORLD
# OF PLANTS

**World Book, Inc.**
a Scott Fetzer company
Chicago

## Childcraft—The How and Why Library

(Reg. U.S. Pat. and T.M. Off.—Marca Registrada)
© 2000 World Book, Inc. All rights reserved. This volume may not
be reproduced in whole or in part in any form without prior written
permission from the publisher.

World Book, Inc.
233 N. Michigan Avenue
Chicago, IL 60601

© 1996, 1995, 1994, 1993, 1991, 1990, 1989, 1987, 1986, 1985
World Book, Inc. © 1982, 1981, 1980, 1979, World Book-Childcraft
International, Inc. © 1976, 1974, 1973, 1971, 1970, 1969, 1968, 1965,
1964 Field Enterprises Educational Corporation.

International Copyright © 1996, 1995, 1994, 1993, 1991, 1990, 1989,
1987, 1986, 1985 World Book, Inc. International Copyright © 1982,
1981, 1980, 1979 World Book-Childcraft International, Inc. International
Copyright © 1976, 1974, 1973, 1971, 1970, 1969, 1968, 1965, 1964
Field Enterprises Educational Corporation.

Childcraft—The How and Why Library  ISBN 0-7166-0197-4
The World of Plants  ISBN 0-7166-0154-0
Library of Congress Catalog Card Number 98-75114
Printed in the United States of America
1  2  3  4  5  6  7  8  9  06  05  04  03  02  01  00

**For information on other World Book products,
visit our Web site at www.worldbook.com
For information on sales to schools and libraries in the
United States, call 1-800-975-3250.
For information on sales to schools and libraries in
Canada, call 1-800-837-5365.**

# Contents

**Know It All!** boxes have fun-filled facts.

Each activity has a number. The higher the number, the more adult help you may need.

An activity that has this colorful border is a little more complex than one without the border.

# Introduction

Think of a breezy meadow. Let your mind drift to a shady forest. Imagine sand drifting across a desert or a breeze running through a farmer's field of corn. Then picture strands of ivy creeping around a pot on a window sill. All of these scenes include plants!

This book, *The World of Plants,* invites you to learn all about these wonderful living things. In it, you will discover how plants live and grow, and where to find them. You will learn about the important things plants do for people, and what things people do for plants.

There are many features in this book to help you find your way through it. The boxes marked **Know It All!** have fun-filled facts. Look for the words **Try This!** over a colored ball. The activity that follows offers a way to learn more about plants. For example, you can grow your own sunflowers.

As you read this book, you will see that some words are printed in bold type, **like this.** These are words that might be new to you. You can find the meanings and pronunciations of these words in the

**Glossary** at the back of the book. Turn to the **Index** to look up page numbers of subjects that interest you the most.

If you enjoy learning about plants, find out more about them in other resources. Here are just a few. Check them out at a bookstore or at your local or school library.

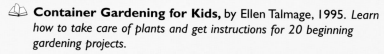 **Container Gardening for Kids,** by Ellen Talmage, 1995. *Learn how to take care of plants and get instructions for 20 beginning gardening projects.*

**Crinkleroot's Guide to Knowing the Trees,** by Jim Arnosky, 1992. *Crinkleroot, a fictitious character who lives in the forest, takes you on a walk through the woods and teaches you many things about trees.*

**Fly Traps! Plants that Bite Back,** by Martin Jenkins, 1996. *This book will introduce you to Venus's-flytrap and other insect-eating flora.*

**From Seed to Plant,** by Gail Gibbons, 1991. *Written in simple language and well illustrated for the very youngest gardners, this book explains how seeds become plants.*

**Gardening Wizardry for Kids,** by Patricia Kite, 1995. *Learn a lot about common fruits, vegetables, and herbs, and get step-by-step instructions for experiments and crafts projects.*

**KinderGARDEN,**
http://aggie-horticulture.tamu.edu/Kindergarden/ index.html
*This is a Web introduction to the many things kids can do with plants.*

**Life Cycle of a Bean,** by Angela Royston, 1998. *This book, written for the beginning young gardner, takes you week by week through the growing cycle of a bean seed.*

**The Magic School Bus Inside a Beehive,** by Joanna Cole, 1996. *You have probably seen bees in your flower garden, but do you know why they are there and what they do after they leave? This book will tell you.*

**National Audubon Society First Field Guide to Wildflowers,** by Susan Hood, 1998. *Take this book along when you go on your next hike and see how many wildflowers you can identify.*

**The Visual Dictionary of Plants,** by Simone End and John Woodcock, 1992. *Beautifully illustrated, this book graphically defines the parts of all kinds of plant life.*

Wonderful plants are found all around the world. Here is just a peek at some of the special plants you'll meet in this book. The map shows you one place in the world where each fantastic plant can be found. Turn to the page numbers listed to find out more!

ARCTIC OCEAN

**North America** • • • • • • • • • • • • • • • •
Bristlecone pine, p. 43
Corn plant, p. 90-93
Joshua tree, p. 78
Redwood, p. 38
Saguaro cactus, p. 34
Venus's-flytrap, p. 49
Yucca plant, p. 78

PACIFIC OCEAN

ATLANTIC OCEAN

**South America** • • • • • • • • • • • • • • • •
Cannonball tree, p. 75
Monkey puzzle tree, p. 39
Ombu tree, p.177
Pampas grass, p. 62-63
Passion-flower, p. 13, 74
Potato plant, p. 32, 97
Rubber tree, p. 108-109

INDIAN
OCEAN

tulips

# The Life of a Plant

**D**o you know how plants differ from other living things? Or what a leaf does?

Have you ever wondered why some trees stay green all year, while others change colors and then lose their leaves? Do you know how new plants are made?

Read on to learn all about the fascinating lives of plants. Some of what you find out will surprise you!

marigolds

saguaro cactus

cone

# What Is a Living Thing?

**D**o you know the difference between a living thing and a nonliving thing? You are a living thing. And so are puppies, trees, and mushrooms. Bicycles, rocks, shoes, and tennis balls are nonliving things.

How do you tell living things from nonliving things? All living things have certain features in common. Almost all living things must have food, water, and air. And they are made up of tiny units called **cells** (sehls). Living things also **reproduce** (REE pruh DOOS). They can make new living things just like themselves.

These tiny bacteria are part of the protist kingdom.

Mushrooms are part of the fungi kingdom.

**All of these are living things.**

These tiny living things are part of the kingdom of prokaryotes.

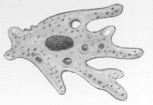

The many, many types of living things are also different from one another in important ways. Scientists separate all living things into large groups called **kingdoms.** Each kingdom is made up of living things that are similar to one another. Each kingdom is different from the other kingdoms.

Most scientists say there are five main kingdoms. Animals make up one of the kingdoms. Most animals move around and get their food by eating other living things. Plants make up another kingdom. The plant kingdom is important to the other kingdoms because plants create the food that most other living things need. The other kingdoms include **organisms** such as **fungi** (FUHN jy) and **algae** (AL jee).

These living things belong to the plant kingdom.

Spiders and tigers belong to the animal kingdom.

# What Is a Plant?

tiger lily

wheat

**I**f someone asked you to name a plant, you might say, "a tree." You'd probably think of many other green and leafy living things, too. But not all plants are green and leafy. Most are, but not all.

So what makes a plant a plant?

Plants usually spend their whole lives rooted to one place. They can't move around like animals. Most plants produce seeds to make new plants.

oak tree

pine tree

Plants also have special kinds of cells. Plant cells have tough, thick walls made of **cellulose** (SEHL yuh lohs). And most plants contain a special substance called **chlorophyll** (KLAWR uh fihl). Plants use chlorophyll to make their own food with the help of water, air, and sunlight.

**cactus**

**passion flower**

**firethorn**

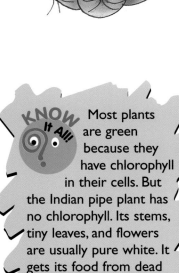

**KNOW It All!** Most plants are green because they have chlorophyll in their cells. But the Indian pipe plant has no chlorophyll. Its stems, tiny leaves, and flowers are usually pure white. It gets its food from dead plant roots.

# Kinds of Plants

**P**lants are divided into groups.

Almost all plants belong to the group called seed plants. They're called seed plants because they make seeds that grow into new plants.

Most seed plants are flowering plants. Flowering plants make their seeds inside flowers. By far, most plants in the world are flowering plants. Other seed plants make their seeds inside cones. Cone-bearing plants are called **conifers** (KAHN uh fuhrz). These plants include such trees as pines, spruces,

Marigolds make their seeds in their flowers.

Gingko trees have been around since the time of the dinosaurs. They make their seeds in cones.

gingkoes

A tree fern does not grow from a seed. It grows from a spore.

and firs. Plants called **cycads** (SY kadz) and **gingkoes** (GIHNG kohz) also are cone-bearing plants. These types of plants have been around for millions of years.

Other plant groups use tiny cells called **spores** (spawrs), not seeds, to make new plants. Spore-making plants include ferns, horsetails, and mosses.

Ferns have feathery leaves called fronds. Their spores form on the undersides of the fronds. Horsetails have tall, green stems with a cap on top. They have long, thin leaves. Moss grows like a soft, green furry coat on a tree trunk or a rock. Moss is made up of thousands of tiny plants growing very close together.

**fern leaf with spores**

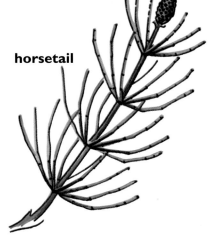

**horsetail**

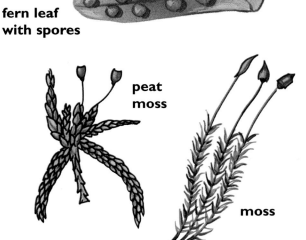

**peat moss**

**moss**

15

# Roots, Stems, and Leaves

**P**lants have many different parts. Many have roots, stems, and leaves. All the parts work together to help the plant live and grow. Not every plant has all these parts, but most do.

Roots grow from the bottom of the plant down into the ground and spread out. Like sponges, roots soak up water and **minerals** for the plant. Roots are anchors too. By growing down and spreading out in the ground, they hold a plant firmly in place.

Stems support a plant's leaves and hold them toward the light. Flowers grow from the stems. Water and minerals travel to the rest of the plant through tiny tubes in the stems. The trunk of a tree is a big stem.

Leaves make food for the plant. They use the energy of sunlight to change air, water, and minerals into sugar and starch. Leaves grow in many

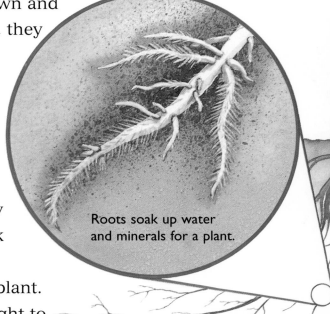

Roots soak up water and minerals for a plant.

shapes and sizes. Some are broad and flat. Others are long and thin. Some leaves have smooth edges. The edges of other leaves are jagged or wavy. And some leaves look like needles or spines.

Leaves make food for the plant.

A plant's stem supports its leaves and holds them toward the light.

After leaves fall, you can see spots on the stem where they were attached.

KNOW It All! Mosses and related plants called liverworts and hornworts have no roots. Instead, they have hairy growths. These growths hold the plant in the soil and take in water and food.

# What Makes Leaves Green?

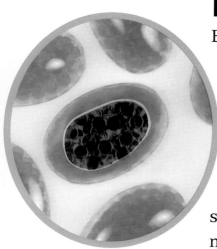

Plant cells contain chlorophyll, the green substance that helps the plant make food.

**L**eaves don't seem to do anything at all. But if you could become tiny enough to peek *inside* a leaf—you would have a surprise!

Sunlight comes into a leaf through the leaf's skin. Inside, the leaves have a wonderful green substance called chlorophyll. The chlorophyll catches some of the sunlight that falls on the leaf. At the same time, air comes into the leaf through many tiny openings. And water moves up from the roots below.

Leaves are like little food factories. Using sunlight for energy, the chlorophyll changes water and a gas from the air into food for the plant.

TRY THIS!
1

Discover why plants stay green. When the weather is warm and sunny, and the grass is not too dry, put a stainless steel or pottery bowl upside down on a patch of grass so that the grass won't get any sun. (Make sure you get permission from the owner of the grass first!) Leave the bowl for about 5 days. No peeking! Then lift the bowl and look at the grass. How is it different from the grass that was in the sun?

As the plant makes food, it gives off gases.

Sunlight passes through the clear skin of a leaf.

Water passes along the stem and into the leaf.

The sugars are the plant's food. They are stored in these cells

Air enters the leaf through tiny openings.

A leaf is like a small food factory.

Besides green, leaves have other colors, such as yellow and orange. In summer, the green chlorophyll covers the other colors. In the autumn, it sometimes fades. Then you see the other colors.

# What Are Seeds?

A seed is a baby plant and a bundle of food all wrapped up in a package.

Different kinds of plants have different kinds of seeds. Some seeds are as big as a baseball. Others are smaller than a grain of sand. Some are round, some are flat, some are long and thin. But in every kind of seed a baby plant, with its store of food, is waiting to grow.

In places that have cold winters, springtime is come-to-life time for seeds. Water from melting snow and spring rains sinks into the earth and soaks into

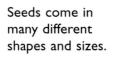

Seeds come in many different shapes and sizes.

the seed. The seed's tough shell—the cover of the package—becomes soft. The food inside the shell swells up with water. Then the shell bursts open.

The baby plant pushes out. It uses its store of food to begin growing. A tiny root pushes down into the ground in search of water. A tiny stem grows up through the soil in search of sunlight.

As the plant grows, it uses its store of food. When it pokes its head above the ground into the sunshine, the plant begins to make its own food. It makes food out of sunlight, air, and water that its roots find.

KNOW It All!
The world's largest seed grows as big as a basketball. It is the coco-de-mer, or double coconut. The coco-de-mer grows in the Seychelles, an island group in the Indian Ocean.

## How a seed grows

The seed bursts open. Out comes a tiny root.

As the root grows down, the stem pushes up.

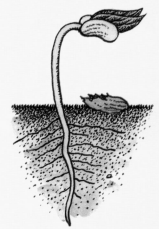

The first leaves begin to make food for the plant.

21

# Seeds on the Move

If a seed grew close to its parent, it probably would be in the shade. It could not get the sunlight it needs to grow. It would not have enough space to grow, either. Somehow, the seed must get to a place where it can grow. Luckily, seeds have many ways of doing this.

Dandelion seeds float through the air like parachutes.

Some seeds, such as maple tree "whirligigs," float on the wind. Their "wings" carry them a long way. Other seeds catch a ride with animals. When animals eat fruit, they eat the seeds along with it, and the seeds pass through the animal's body. The animal may travel far before dropping the seeds. Other seeds, such as those of bur marigolds, needlegrass, and beggar-ticks, grow inside fruits that stick to things. They hitchhike on the fur of passing animals until they are brushed off.

Some fruits actually explode. Dry peapods split open, hurling their seeds in all directions. Touch-me-not plants have pods that fly open at the slightest movement. And the squirting cucumber shoots out seeds in a jet of liquid.

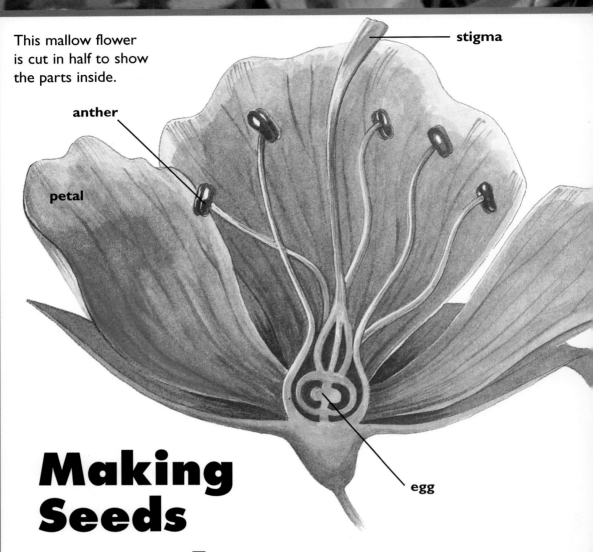

This mallow flower is cut in half to show the parts inside.

stigma

anther

petal

egg

# Making Seeds

**A**ll seed plants have special seed-making parts. Most seed plants make their seeds inside flowers. The seed-making parts of a flower include long stalks. Some stalks have enlarged tips called **anthers**. Anthers make a golden dust called **pollen**. Other stalks have a sticky top called a **stigma**.

**seed-making cones**

**pollen-making cones**

A seed starts to form when pollen from one flower falls onto the stigma of another flower of the same kind. The pollen travels down the stalk until it reaches a tiny egg. The pollen joins with the egg, which then grows into a seed.

Other seed plants make their seeds inside cones. There are two kinds of cones. One is small and delicate. It makes pollen. The other kind of cone is covered with wood scales and makes eggs. A seed starts to form when pollen blows from the delicate cones and lands on the scaly cones. The pollen and the eggs join. The scales close around the developing seeds. When the seeds are ripe, the scales open up again, and the seeds fall from the cones.

# Traveling Pollen

A bright flower with sweet nectar attracts a hungry hummingbird.

**P**lants can't move around. So how do you think they spread their pollen to make seeds? Most plants use the wind or animals to help them **pollinate** (PAHL uh nayt).

All grasses and many trees, such as hazels and birches, scatter their pollen on the wind. The anthers of these plants hang out of the flower so that a puff of wind can carry away the pollen. The stigmas of these plants also hang out of the flower. They can catch the pollen as it blows past.

The head and legs of this bee are covered in pollen.

In Australia, banksia plants are sometimes pollinated by honey possums.

Insects, birds, and bats help spread the pollen of some plants. The flowers of these plants attract the animals. Many such flowers are full of sweet-tasting juice called **nectar** (NEHK tuhr) that bees and other animals like to eat. Some flowers "advertise" their supply of nectar with strong scents and bright colors.

When an animal visits a flower to sip the nectar, pollen brushes off onto its body. Then, when it visits the next flower, the pollen on its body brushes off into that flower.

# The Life Cycle of a Seed Plant

Like all living things, plants start their lives, grow, reproduce, and die. These steps make up a plant's life cycle.

A seed plant begins when a seed **germinates** (JUHR muh nayts), or sprouts. A tiny root pushes down into the ground in search of water. A tiny stem pushes up through the soil in search of sunlight. A new plant soon pokes its head above the ground.

The plant grows. Its roots take in water. Its leaves make food. After a time, the plant is fully grown. Small plants may become fully grown in a few weeks or months. A huge tree may take hundreds of years or more.

growth

germination

When a plant is ready to reproduce, it makes flowers or cones. The flowers and cones make pollen and eggs. The pollen and eggs join. Then new seeds form. Some seeds will be eaten by animals. Others will land in a place where they cannot grow. But some seeds will find a spot where the soil, water, and temperature are just right. These seeds will germinate, and the life cycle will begin again.

When a plant grows old, it dies. Its roots, stem, and leaves become part of the soil.

TRY THIS!

1

Make your own hanging garden. Wet a piece of paper towel. Put it in a plastic bag and place lima beans, sunflower seeds, or radish seeds between the towel and the bag. Soak larger seeds in water overnight before you put them in the bag. This will loosen their seed coat and help them to sprout faster. Seal the bag shut and tape it to a sunny window. Watch your seeds germinate.

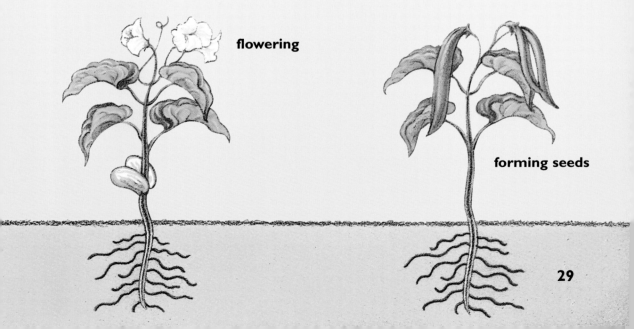

flowering

forming seeds

# Make a Model Flower

**N**ow that you know the seed-making parts of a flower, make your own flower out of paper and pipe cleaners.

## What To Do:

**1.** Use a pencil to trace the patterns from the opposite page onto tracing paper. Cut them out of the tracing paper.

**2.** Trace the single leaf and the group of leaves onto green paper. Trace the single leaf twice so that you'll have two copies of it. Trace the petals onto red paper. Cut out all of the shapes.

## You Will Need:

tracing paper

a pencil

scissors

red and green
   construction paper

modeling clay

a bendable straw

clear tape

six 3-inch
   (7.5-centimeter)
   pieces of yellow
   pipe cleaner

**3.** Use the pencil carefully to poke a hole into the center of the cutout of the group of leaves. Then poke a hole in the center in the group of petals.

**4.** Form a lump of modeling clay into a ball. Stick the straw into the clay, with the bent end at the top.

**5.** Slide the cutouts of the leaves and the petals onto the straw. Hold them near the top of the straw. Keep them in place by putting a small piece of modeling clay around the straw just below the cutouts.

**group of petals**

**6.** Make a bend in a pipe cleaner, close to one end. Curl the other end into a loop. Repeat with the rest of the pipe cleaners. Then stick the pipe cleaners into the end of the straw.

**7.** Tape the two loose leaves near the center of the straw. Your flower is complete!

Make more flowers and create a garden.

**group of leaves**

**single leaf**

# Making Plants Without Seeds

**N**ot all plants have to make seeds to grow new plants. Some plants can make copies of themselves without the help of another plant.

The byrophyllum grows new plants around the edges of its leaves.

If you plant a potato, a new plant will sprout from it! A potato is a **tuber.** New stems sprout from a tuber's bud, called an eye.

potato

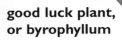

good luck plant, or byrophyllum

The leaves and stems of some new plants grow out of underground buds called **bulbs.** Flowers such as lilies, tulips, and crocuses grow from bulbs. Onion and garlic plants have bulbs you can eat!

Some plants grow copies of themselves by sending off shoots. Mint and some kinds of grasses have underground stems from which new plants will grow. Strawberry plants produce stems called **runners** that grow sideways. New plants grow on the runners and root themselves wherever they touch the ground.

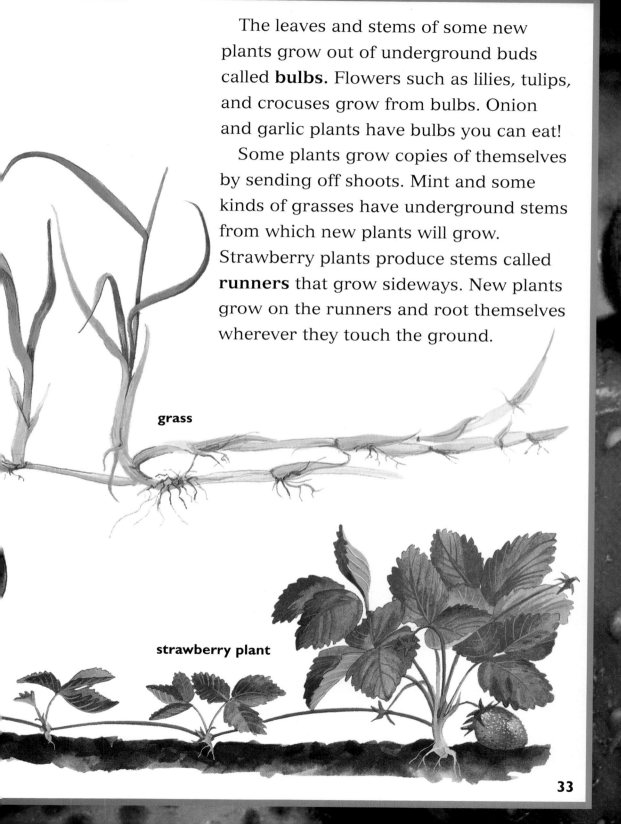

grass

strawberry plant

# The Largest Plants

The leaves of a cycad tree grow in a circle at the end of the stem.

The saguaro cactus is actually a tree, but it has sharp spines instead of flat, green leaves.

**C**an you climb a corn plant or a tulip? Can you swing from a daisy? Of course not! But a tree is a different matter entirely.

Trees are tall, sturdy plants with woody stems called trunks. Branches grow from the trunk, usually quite far off the ground. It's the trunk that makes a tree so strong. The trunk supports the tree.

The trunk also has several layers, each with an important job to do. Tree trunks are covered with a tough outer skin. Most trees have a hard, dry skin called bark. The bark protects the soft inside part of the tree. The next layer carries food made by the leaves to other parts of the tree. Next to this layer is the part of the trunk that makes the bark and new wood. Farther inside is the wood. Some wood carries water around the tree. The inner wood helps support the tree.

Most palm trees have a branchless trunk topped by a crown of huge leaves.

Tree trunks are made up of several layers, *right,* each with its own job to do. Water and food move from the roots and the leaves through the trunk.

KNOW It All!

In regions where trees make a new layer of wood once a year, the layers form a series of annual rings. After the tree has been cut down, each year's layer of wood can be seen as a ring. A tree with 50 rings has lived for 50 years. The rings also reveal the tree's life story. Narrow rings show that there was not much water or sunlight that year. Wider rings mean more water, sunlight, and growth.

# Broadleaf Trees

**M**any broadleaf trees lose their leaves once a year and later grow new leaves. These trees are called **deciduous** (dih SIHJ oo uhs) trees. Oaks, maples, lindens, and many other types of trees are deciduous.

In places that have cold winters and warm summers, most deciduous trees lose their leaves in autumn. Leaves need water to stay alive and to make food. A tree gets water from the soil. But in winter, the water in the soil turns to ice. The roots can't take in this frozen water. There is no water for the trees.

In late summer, the tree begins to prepare for winter. A thick layer grows where each leaf's stem is attached to the twig. Water can no longer get into the leaves. The leaves dry up, fall to the ground, and die.

In springtime, the ground warms up. The ice melts. The soil is wet again. Then a tree's roots start taking in water, and the tree grows new leaves.

But not all broadleaf trees are deciduous. In warmer parts of the world, broadleaf trees stay green all year. They are called broadleaf evergreens. They lose just a few leaves at a time. The eucalyptus, or gum, trees of Australia are broadleaf evergreens.

In summer, water reaches all parts of the leaf through the stem.

In autumn, a cork layer keeps water from reaching the leaf.

The leaf falls off, leaving a scar.

# Needleleaf Trees

The kinds of trees that are often used as Christmas trees are needleleaf trees. They are called needleleaf trees because their leaves are thin and sharp, like needles. Pines, spruces, redwoods, and hemlocks are all needleleaf trees.

Most needleleaf trees are green all year. They are called evergreens. They don't change color and lose all their leaves at a certain time each year as deciduous trees do. Instead, they lose a few needles at a time, all year around.

**Douglas fir**

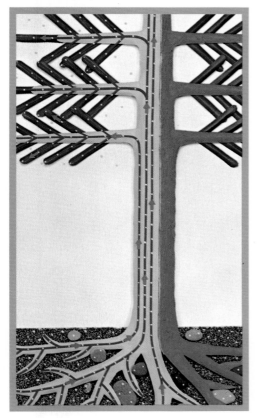

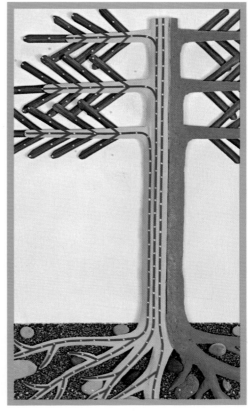

Arrows show water *(dots)* going up to an evergreen tree's needles in summer. Some water is lost into the air, but not as much as other kinds of trees lose.

No water comes up from the roots in winter. No water moves through the tree. But the needles stay green. They live on the water that is still in them.

Needles are very tough. They don't freeze in winter, and they don't lose water as quickly as other kinds of leaves do. By holding on to the water they have, needleleaf trees stay alive and green all winter.

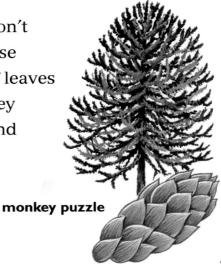

**monkey puzzle**

The world's tallest trees, *left,* are California's redwoods. Redwoods may grow as tall as a 37-story building.

# Watering Plants

**H**ave you ever seen firefighters using a fire hose? The hose looks stiff and fat while water is running through it. But when the fire is put out and the firefighters turn off the water, the empty hose is limp.

Many plants are something like a fire hose. As long as their roots keep pumping water, their stems and leaves stand up straight and stiff. But a plant loses water through its leaves. If the plant doesn't get enough water to replace

the lost water, it will soon flop over, just like an empty fire hose. Perhaps you've seen this happen to potted plants. They begin to droop when they need water.

Desert plants are good at collecting and storing water.

Plants that live in deserts, where there is very little water, have special ways of collecting and storing water. For example, the roots of some cactus plants grow down deep or spread out very far to find water. Cactuses store the water in their thick, fleshy stems. When there is no rain, they live off the water they have stored.

**TRY THIS!**

**1** See how water leaves a plant. On a sunny day, when the soil around a plant is dry on top, put a glass jar over the plant. Wait an hour and check the inside of the jar. What do you see? You should see drops of water or mist. The water has come out of the plant through tiny holes in its leaves.

# How Long Do Plants Live?

**S**ome plants live for only one year. These plants are called **annuals.** The seeds of annuals sprout in the spring. A new plant grows. The plant flowers and makes new seeds in summer. When winter comes, the plant dies, leaving seeds in the ground to germinate in spring.

Some plants seem to die in winter. Their leaves fall off and their stems look dry and lifeless. But in the spring they start growing again. These plants are called **perennials** (puh REHN ee uhlz). Perennial plants grow back year after year.

A rose plant grows year after year.

A foxglove lives for two years.

A tulip grows year after year.

A **biennial** (by EHN ee uhl) plant lives for two years. The first year, it grows leaves and shoots. As it grows, it stores food, often in a swollen root. When winter comes, the leaves and stems die. The next spring, the plant grows again. It flowers and makes seeds, using the food it had stored up the previous year. Then it dies.

A morning glory lives for a year.

Some of the oldest known plants are the bristlecone pine trees of California. Some bristlecone pine trees are nearly 5,000 years old.

KNOW It All!

43

# Poisonous Plants

**M**any kinds of berries and seeds are poisonous! People have died from eating mistletoe berries, yew berries, and castor beans. Belladonna, or deadly nightshade, has green or black berries—both are dangerous! Never eat a berry, seed, or nut unless a grown-up says it is safe.

Some plants make you itch and burn if you touch them. You can avoid them if you know what they look like. Poison sumac has white berries that hang down. Poison ivy grows as a vine, with leaves in groups of three. That's where the cautionary rhyme "Leaves of three, let it be" came from. Nettles have bristles that can make you itch.

Some of the most beautiful plants are poisonous. The oleander can sicken or even kill a person who eats it. Some plants have both poisonous and nonpoisonous parts. Rhubarb stems are good to eat, but eating rhubarb leaves can make you very ill!

mistletoe

yew berries

castor beans

poison ivy

oleander

deadly nightshade

rhubarb

# Strange and Unusual Plants

**dodder**

If you think that all plants look and act alike, you're in for a surprise. Plants come in more shapes and colors and live in more places than you can imagine. They have some unusual ways to get their food and water, too.

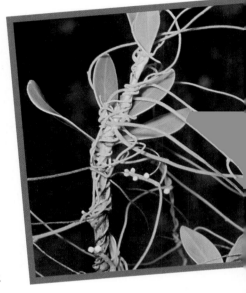

The cushion plant is bright green in spring and summer. But in winter, it turns white and looks like soft wool.

New Zealand has a plant that looks like a soft cushion. It's called a cushion plant. It's made up of thousands of tiny stems with millions of little leaves. The leaves are covered with the tiny hairs. The stems are so close together that the plant looks like one big green cushion. In winter, the plant turns white, giving it a woolly look.

Some plants live by "stealing" food or water from other plants. When the dodder sprouts from the ground, it begins to grow toward the nearest plant. The dodder soon wraps itself around the other plant. It gets its food and water by sucking them out of the other plant. Mistletoe also gets its water this way. Mistletoe grows on many kinds of trees, with its roots sunk deep into the tree's branches.

Before the leaves of the sensitive plant are touched, they are wide open, *top*. But when the plant is touched, its leaves suddenly fold up and droop, *bottom*.

Some plants even move! They don't actually get up and walk around, but they open and close, or fold and unfold. For example, if you touch the leaves of the sensitive plant, they will fold up suddenly and droop. Then, in a short time, they will unfold and straighten up again.

# Plants That Eat Insects

**Y**ou probably know that many insects eat plants. But did you know that some plants eat insects? These plants include the sundew and the Venus's-flytrap. They need to eat insects because their soil does not have enough food to help them grow.

The leaves of sundew plants are covered with little hairs. On each hair there is a drop of sticky liquid. These drops glitter like dew in the sunshine and attract insects. When an insect touches one of the drops, it is stuck! Then all the hairs slowly fold in around the insect. They push the insect down against the leaf. A juice oozes out of the leaf and **digests** (dy JEHSTS) the insect.

This aphid has been caught by the sticky hairs of the sundew plant.

**sundew**

The leaves of the Venus's-flytrap snap shut on insects.

The leaves of the Venus's-flytrap work just like traps. They can open and close like clam shells. Little "claws" surround the edge of each leaf, and tiny hairs grow on the inside. When a fly or other insect lands on a leaf and touches one of the hairs, the leaves quickly close like a trap. Then the plant digests its meal.

# Fungi

**F**ungi are living things that are a lot like plants. They grow almost everywhere in nature, including the air. They don't move around, but they do reproduce. Scientists once called fungi "plants," but fungi cannot make their own food. They get their food from dead plants and animals. So today, experts put these living things in a group of their own. Mushrooms, mold, and yeast are types of fungi.

When mold grows on an apple, *below*, it spoils the apple. But some molds give the food they grow on its taste, like the Roquefort cheese above.

Mushrooms and molds grow from tiny cells called spores. Spores float on the air like dust. When a spore lands on bread or something else it can use as food, it begins to grow. It sends out many tiny threads. Some of these threads grow down, like roots. Others grow upward, like stems. Bunches of these threads form the spots you see on moldy fruit or cheese.

A baker uses yeast, *inset*, to make bread fluffy. As the tiny cells take in sugar, they change part of it to gas. The gas makes the bread airy and fluffy.

Yeast cells look like drops of jelly. They're so tiny you can't see them without a microscope. When a yeast cell takes in food, such as sugar, it swells up and splits into two new cells. Then, each new cell takes in food, swells up, and splits in two. Soon, there are millions of new yeast cells. People put yeast in bread dough to help make the bread fluffy.

Many mushrooms look like open umbrellas. They are often found growing around fallen trees and dead leaves. Below are several kinds of mushrooms.

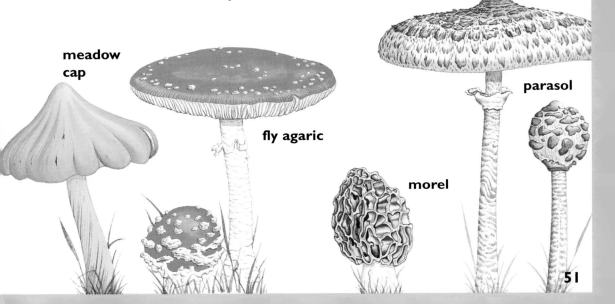

meadow cap

fly agaric

morel

parasol

51

# Algae— Almost Plants

**S**eaweeds look like plants. They even make their own food from sunlight, like plants do. But seaweeds are not plants. They do not have true roots, stems, leaves, or flowers. They are special types of living things called algae.

Seaweeds are built well for a life in the sea. They are soft and flexible and can sway in the water without being torn apart. Some seaweeds use a rootlike anchor to cling to rocks, shells, or the sea floor. Some have gas-filled swellings to

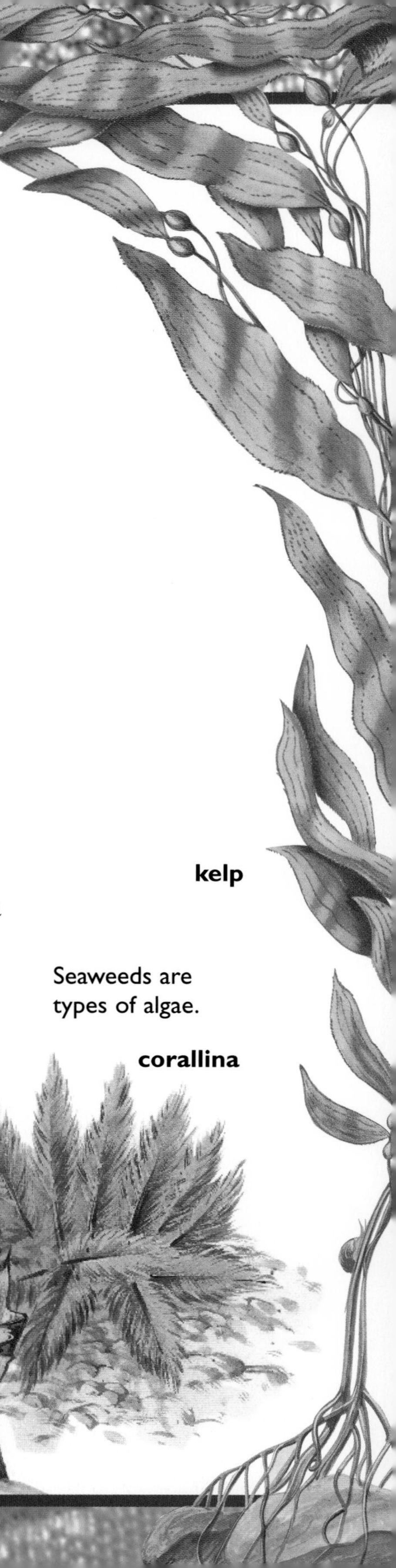

**kelp**

Seaweeds are types of algae.

**corallina**

**oarweed**

**sea lettuce**

keep afloat. Sargassum weed floats in large masses in the ocean. Eel grass grows in thick beds at the muddy bottom of shallow waters. It looks like a field of waving grass along the shore. There are also underwater forests of kelp that grow up from the shallow sea floor.

Some algae swim by wiggling two threads.

Some kinds of algae are so small that you need a microscope to see them. And some of them can move around. They do this by beating little hairs that grow from their surface. Sometimes these tiny algae cling together in chains or gather into jellylike balls.

Sometimes 32 of these tiny algae form a ball and live in it together.

one-celled algae

water lilies

vine

mountain
avens

# Nature's Neighbors

**P**eople often live and work together in communities, such as cities and towns. Plants live in communities too. Plants live together in places that have the kind of weather—sunlight, temperature, and moisture—and soil that they need.

Plants that live in a swamp are the ones that grow best in a wet place. Plants that live in a desert are the ones that grow best in a very dry place. Swamp plants and desert plants could rarely be neighbors. They belong to different plant communities. Other plant communities live in forests, grasslands, and tundras.

oak

# Where Plants Change Clothes

In spring, birds appear and build nests.

In autumn, squirrels collect nuts in the forest.

Rabbits stay active in a mild winter.

**D**o the trees where you live "change their clothes" during the year—from light green buds in the springtime, to dark green leaves in the summer, to reds, golds or purples in the autumn? If so, then they make up a **temperate** (TEHM puhr iht) forest community.

*Temperate* means "mild." Temperate forests grow where summers aren't too hot and winters aren't too cold, and where the ground gets just about the same amount of moisture all year.

In spring, wildflowers bloom in a temperate forest. Then trees and bushes bud. Birds build nests. In summer, fruits and nuts grow and ripen. The woodland is filled with birds, squirrels, raccoons, and many other small animals.

In autumn, the leaves change color. Most birds fly south for winter. Snakes, turtles, frogs, and many insects hibernate. So do some furry animals. But if the winter is mild, the animals stay active.

oak

maple

hazel

# Plants of the Temperate Forest Community

**T**emperate forests have many kinds of trees, shrubs, and other plants. They provide animals with shelter, food, and places to bring up their young. Broadleaf trees, such as oaks, maples, elms, lindens, beeches, and hornbeams, are the most important plants in these woodlands. Many smaller plants and shrubs grow on the forest floor. Wildflowers often cover the woodland floor in spring.

columbine

skunk cabbage

lesser celandine

hepaticas

bluebell

# Giant Lawns

**G**rasses don't need as much water as trees and bushes do. So grasses grow well in wide, open places that are too dry for most trees but not dry enough to be deserts. These places are like giant lawns. They are called grasslands.

Grasslands are special in another way. They sometimes burn up naturally—and this helps them stay healthy! The fire burns the plants to the ground. The ashes feed the new plants that replace them.

Most big animals that live on grasslands, such as zebras, eat grass. Most small animals, such as rabbits, eat plant leaves and seeds. There are also meat-eating animals, such as foxes, snakes, and in some places, lions and leopards. Many meat-eating birds, such as hawks, hunt on grasslands.

It's hard for a hunted animal to hide in a grassland. The ground is low and flat, and there are few trees or bushes. Many animals crouch near the ground. Some, such as rabbits and zebras, can save themselves by running fast or skillfully. Others dig tunnels in which to hide.

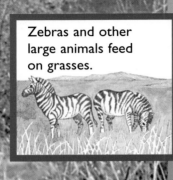

Zebras and other large animals feed on grasses.

Hawks and other meat-eating birds hunt small grassland animals.

Prairie dogs and other small grassland animals eat leaves and seeds.

# Plants of the Grassland Community

gray-headed coneflower

**T**he grass on a grassland may be short or tall, depending on how much moisture there is. Hardly any trees or bushes grow on a grassland, but there are many small plants with white or colored flowers.

In North America, grasslands with tall grasses are called **prairies.** In South America, they're called **pampas** (PAHM puhs). Parts of North America once had prairies where the grasses grew 6 feet (1.8 meters) tall or more.

In Africa and Australia, the grassland is quite dry and the grasses are short. In Africa, there are **savannas** (suh VAN uhz) that have scattered trees and clumps of grasses. Australian grassland is covered with tough Mitchell grass and kangaroo grass. Acacia bushes grow among these grasses. In Argentina and Russia, grasslands called **steppes** (stehps) also have short grasses.

Indian grass

rattlesnake or quaking grass

Mitchell grass

Many grassland plants have special features that help them survive dry conditions. Soft hairs on their leaves and stems help them hold water. Their roots spread out far and wide so they can collect water when rain falls.

**TRY THIS!**

**1**

Grow grassy hair. Take a disposable cup and draw a fun face on it. Fill the cup with soil. Plant grass seeds. Keep the soil moist and in a sunny window. Watch the hair grow!

purple prairie clover

pampas grass

kangaroo grass

red top grass

hairy spinifex

# Watery Places

There are two main types of water communities—freshwater and saltwater. Freshwater communities include ponds, lakes, rivers, and marshes. In summer, some ponds are so covered with plants that you can hardly see the water underneath. Saltwater communities are found along seacoasts. There, the tides rise and fall, so the plants are sometimes above water and sometimes underwater.

Plants that grow in and around watery places give food and shelter to many animals. Grebes and other water birds use these plants to make nests. Muskrats eat plants such as cattails and also use them for building houses. Frogs often fasten their eggs to water plants. When the eggs hatch, the tadpoles use the plants as food. Bass and other big fish hide among water plants. From these hiding places, they dart out to snap up careless frogs and small fish.

Water birds use plants to make nests.

Big fish hide among water plants.

# Plants of Watery Communities

**W**ater plants may grow partly in and partly out of the water. Freshwater plants such as cattails, bulrushes, bur reeds, and papyrus have tough roots that give them a firm grip in the mud. Saltwater plants that do this include cordgrass, sedges, and **mangroves** (MANG grohvz).

Water lilies and lotuses root themselves in the mud at the bottom of a pond and spread their platelike leaves over the surface of the water. The leaves of the

duckweed

lotuses

huge Amazonian water lily grow up to 6 feet (1.8 meters) across.

Other water plants, such as duckweed and frogbit, float on top of the water. Their roots hang down into the water. They do not have stems at all.

Still other water plants live completely underwater. Even plants that live underwater need air. Freshwater plants have special features that enable them to survive. These plants have air spaces in their stems. The air spaces carry air down through the stem to the roots. They also help keep the plant standing up straight in the water.

mangrove

white water lily

papyrus

bulrushes

# The Land of Conifers

In the northern parts of the world, winters are long and cold and summers are cool. Northern lands are home to spruce, firs, and other **conifers**. These trees grow well in cold places.

Conifers grow close together in the northern forests. There are many ponds and lakes. Beavers, muskrats, moose, deer, and water birds live on the many plants that grow around the water. The lynx and the mountain lion are two big cats that live among the conifers.

In winter, it snows heavily in the northern forests. Many birds fly south. Squirrels and bears go to sleep. Other animals, such as elk, stay awake and active all winter. In spring, the snow melts and soaks into the ground. This gives the trees most of the water they need.

Conifers are able to live in many parts of the world. But they do best in cold, northern forest communities.

elk

lynx

# Plants of the Northern Forest Community

**T**he huge northern forests are mostly spruces, firs, pines, and other conifers. These trees can live where the weather is really cold. Their needlelike leaves are tough enough to hold water through the long, dry winter. The

white spruce

juniper

bunchberry

70

**bilberry**

**white birch**

**red pine**

**twinflower**

wind blows through the needles without making the trees sway too much. The trees' sloping shape allows heavy snow to slide off without breaking branches.

Not many small plants grow in the northern forests. The soil is too poor, and there is limited sunlight. But ferns, horsetails, mosses, a few kinds of wildflowers, and such shrubs as bunchberry and cranberry can survive there.

# Rain Forests

Countless animals live in tropical rain forests.

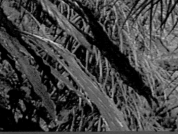

**M**any kinds of trees grow best where it is always wet. So much rain falls in these places that they are known as rain forests. Throughout the year, life is always much the same in a rain forest. Rain storms soak these forests almost every day. The trees are always green.

In tropical rain forests, the air is hot night and day. Millions of animals live in tropical rain forests. The animals are very noisy as they call out in the deep shade. Most of them live in the trees. Monkeys, apes, flying squirrels, anteaters, snakes, insects, and parrots all make their homes in the branches. Animals eat in the trees and make their nests there.

Few animals live on the rain forest floor, where there is less food to be found and more danger from predators. The large trees and their huge leaves block out most of the sunlight and so keep smaller plants from growing.

Not all places called rain forests are hot. The temperate rain forest of the northwest coast of the United States is cool, wet, and green all year around.

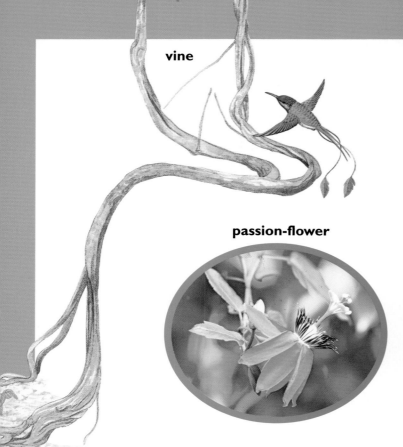

vine

passion-flower

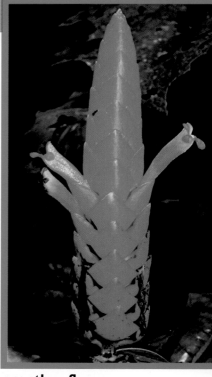

acanthus flower

# Plants of the Rain Forest Community

The rain forest is a woodland of tall trees growing where the weather is warm and wet year-round. Trees in the rain forest stay green all year, and they often grow very tall.

There are three layers to the rain forest. The top layer of branches that extend the highest in the forest make up the **emergent layer** (ih MER juhnt LAY uhr). The main "umbrella" of huge leaves is called the **canopy**. Sometimes there is a lower canopy made up of the leaves of smaller trees.

Many other plants grow on the upper branches of the trees. Vines and plants twine around the trees, climbing up toward the sunlight. Plants such as orchids perch high up on tree branches and trunks. Many flowering plants are brightly colored to attract insects, birds, and other animals that help spread their pollen or seeds.

**cannonball tree**

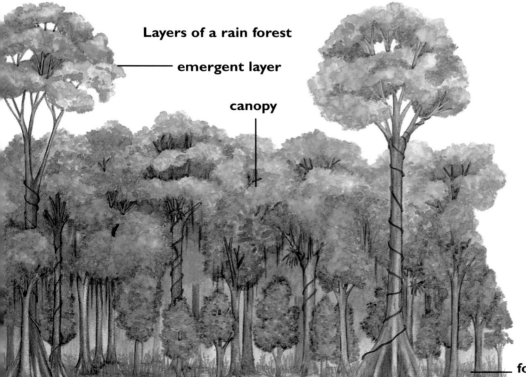

**Layers of a rain forest**

emergent layer

canopy

forest floor

# Where It's Always Dry

**A** desert seems like a tough place for plants to live. There's little water, and the ground is hard and dry. But many plants and animals survive in deserts.

It doesn't rain often in a desert. And when it does, the ground dries quickly. So the roots of most desert plants spread far out just below the surface of the ground. The plants' roots can then catch every drop of water that falls. Most desert plants store up all the water they can get.

During the day, the desert looks lifeless. Most desert animals hide where they can escape the sun's heat—under a rock, underground, or even in a hole in a cactus.

When the sun goes down, a desert quickly cools. Desert rodents look for seeds. Lizards hunt insects. Snakes hunt the rodents and lizards.

It sometimes rains in a desert. When it does, the desert bursts into bloom because there are many seeds in most deserts. But almost all of these plants quickly wither and die as the ground dries again.

During the day, the desert looks hot and lifeless.

As the sun goes down, the desert cools and bursts into life.

# Plants of the Desert Community

Joshua tree

**T**he plants of the desert come in many shapes, sizes, and colors. But they all have one thing in common. They all have ways to survive with little water.

Some desert plants almost stop living between rains. But when the rains come, the plants burst into life. Then they quickly produce seeds before the next long dry spell.

Some plants, like the barrel cactus, swell up to hold a water supply. Before it rains, the barrel cactus looks like a gray lump. But after the rain falls, it is a fat, green ball. Cactuses like this one store water in their stems.

Many animals would like to eat desert plants to get the water inside them. But most desert plants protect their precious supply of water with thousands of prickly spines. These spines also do another

**TRY THIS!**

1

See for yourself why plants like cool nights in the desert. Ask an adult to run warm water over a glass or jar to warm it up. Then put the dry glass upside down on a flat plate. Set it in a cool place overnight. What do you see in the morning?

job. They make shadows. A cactus
creates its own shade by casting
thousands of tiny shadows on itself.

pincushion cactus

candelabra cactus

aloe

welwitschia

pincushion
cactus

stone
plants

# The Frozen North

musk oxen

fox

**F**ar in the north, on the edge of the great sea that surrounds the North Pole, there is a great, flat plain called the **tundra**. Most of the time this plain is bare and frozen. For half the year, days there are nearly all dark and sunless.

In the spring, as the days grow longer, the tundra warms up and the ice melts. Water soaks into the ground. Plants burst into bloom! In summer, the tundra is a busy place. Little lemmings and other animals eat leaves, roots, and seeds. They, in turn, are hunted and eaten by animals such as foxes and wolves.

Winter comes suddenly and lasts a long time in the Arctic. The ground freezes. Snow piles up. Most of the animals leave, but some stay. Lemmings burrow into the ground and live on seeds they have stored away. Herds of musk oxen move from place to place, scraping with their hooves to find food beneath the snow.

bilberries

willows

# Plants of the Tundra Community

**M**ost of the tundra is a treeless plain. Even during the short period of warmer summer days, a fierce and terrible wind blows over the land. So only tough, sturdy plants that grow close to the

**cottongrass**

**sorrel**

**reindeer moss**

ground can live in this community. Birches and willow trees no bigger than bushes grow here and there. But mosses and small flowering plants are the main plants.

# Way Up High

**A** mountain has many kinds of plant communities.

The top of a very high mountain is always covered with ice and snow. No plants grow there.

A little lower on the mountain, the snow melts in summer and many plants bloom.

Some plant-eaters, such as vicuñas in South America and yaks in Tibet, live this high on mountains. Small rodents called alpine marmots live there. So do pikas, which are related to the rabbit.

Lower on the mountain, forests grow. In North America and Europe, you can find bears, deer, elk, foxes, and insects at this level. Trout live in the streams. In eastern Africa, mountain gorillas live in cool mountain forests. Plant-eating animals, such as deer, often move up the slopes in summer and down in winter, to be where food is plentiful.

The plants and animals at the foot of the mountain are the same kinds that live in the surrounding countryside, whether it is forest or desert.

butterflies

snow leopard

85

# Plants of the Mountain Community

**T**he tallest mountains are covered with snow and ice, but smaller mountains are often covered with grasses, forests, or mosses and other small plants. In deserts, mountaintops may be dry and stony.

A little lower on the mountain, small plants grow close to the ground for warmth and protection from the wind. A little farther down is the **timber line.** Above that line, trees cannot grow. Along the timber line, most trees are small and bent. Below the timber line, the trees grow taller and make a forest that covers the sides of the mountain.

**Engelman spruce tree**

**timber line**

**fire lily**

The alpine lily is one of the tallest alpine plants. Its slender stem can bend in the wind, so it isn't damaged in storms. Alpine saxifrage grows into a kind of flat cushion. And edelweiss has a way of keeping itself warm. It is covered with a thick layer of white hairs that act as a coat and keep the heat in.

edelweiss

poplar

Turk's cap lily

alpine rhododendron

alpine saxifrage

mountain avens

seamless thistle

# What Plants Do for Us

**W**e couldn't even breathe without the fresh air plants make! And plants do so much else for us, too. They give us vegetables, fruits, cereals, and most of the other foods we eat. Plants also provide us with wood for building houses and making furniture.

People make cloth—such as cotton and linen for clothes, towels, and sheets—from plants. We get paper, rubber, string, and medicines from plants, too.

Plants also give us pleasure. They are nice to look at, touch, and smell.

food and dyes

wood

cloth

Many favorite foods, such as rice, are made from plants called cereals.

**millet**

# Cereals

For years, our ancestors ate the seeds of wild grasses and chewed the roots of wild plants. Then, about 11,000 years ago, people started to grow the crops they liked best. Ever since, we've been growing and developing all sorts of plants to feed ourselves and our animals.

You probably eat grass every day! When we think of grass, we usually think of the grass in lawns and fields. But rice, wheat, oats, rye, millet, barley, sorghum, and corn are grasses, too.

**sorghum**

These grasses are called **cereals.** And their fruits, the part we eat, are called grains.

Cereals are the most important group of food plants in the world. Without grains, we wouldn't have bread, breakfast cereals, cakes, rice, or popcorn. Grasses also provide food for the cows and sheep that give us milk, cheese, and meat.

rice

oats

A girl in Colombia prepares a thin, corn-meal pancake called a tortilla.

wheat

corn

# The First Corn

*This Native American tale tells how corn came to be.*

**M**any years ago, a boy lived with his grandmother. Every day, the boy hunted and caught a bird. Every evening, his grandmother brought a basket of corn from the storehouse. Then she prepared dinner with the bird and the corn.

One day, the boy glanced into the storehouse and saw it was empty. But that night his grandmother brought a basket of corn as usual. So the next evening the boy followed her to the storehouse. He saw her lean over the basket and rub her hand along her body. Dried corn flowed into the basket.

To North American Indians, corn was a very valuable plant.

corn

Before the boy could run away, she saw
him. "Now that you know my secret, I
must leave you," she said. "But hear me.
When I die, clear a piece of land. Bury my
body in that land, and I will be back to
feed the tribe."

That night, the boy's grandmother died.
In the morning, he cleared the land. As he
pulled her body toward her burial place,
small plants sprang up behind it. The boy
tended the plants. Months later, they were
as tall as a person. Their silky hair was like
his grandmother's. And the plants
produced enough corn for the whole tribe.

# Eating Fruits and Flowers

**F**ruits are really the seed packages of plants. People find lots of fruits delicious. Birds and other creatures think so, too.

Sometimes we eat the whole fruit, seeds and all, but if the seed is too big or tough, we remove it. It's easy to eat the seeds of strawberries, bananas, kiwi, and tomato fruits. But people don't eat the seeds of apples, cherries, peaches, and dates.

dates

tomato

**garden nasturtium**

melon

apple

All these pictures show delicious foods that are seeds, fruits, or flowers.

When you eat lima beans, peas, or lentils, you eat the seeds of fruits. When you eat green beans or French beans, you eat the whole pod, not just the seeds inside it.

Many flowers aren't good to eat, but cauliflower and broccoli are delicious before they come into bloom. The flowers of nasturtiums and violets taste good and make salads even prettier!

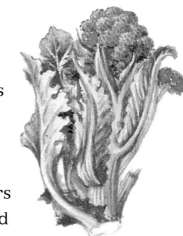

**broccoli**

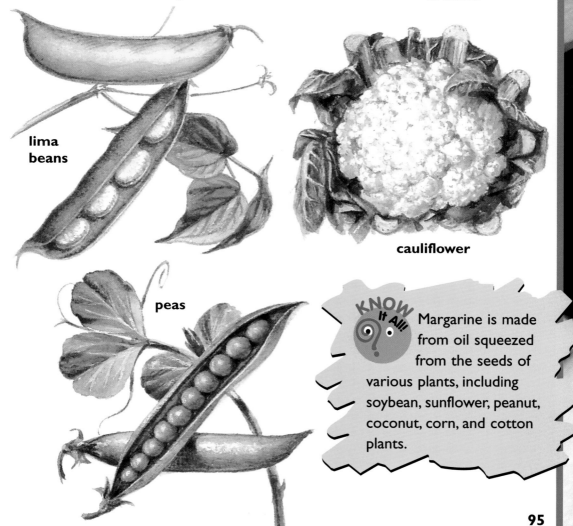

**lima beans**

**cauliflower**

**peas**

**KNOW It All!** Margarine is made from oil squeezed from the seeds of various plants, including soybean, sunflower, peanut, coconut, corn, and cotton plants.

Rhubarb is a vegetable, just like lettuce and cabbage. But only the stems of rhubarb are edible—its leaves are poisonous!

**rhubarb**

All these pictures show delicious foods that are leaves, stems, or roots.

**lettuce**

# Eating Leaves, Stems, and Roots

**W**hat is your favorite food that is a leaf, stem, or root? Lots of plants are grown for their leaves. Lettuce grows in different shapes, from long and tall to

round and fat. Lettuce leaves are popular in salads. Spinach leaves can be eaten raw or cooked. They're full of minerals and vitamins.

Stems make good food, too. Celery stalks can be cooked or eaten raw. Rhubarb stems are delicious in pie. The potato is an underground stem vegetable.

You might think an onion is a root vegetable, but it isn't. The part you eat is really leaves. Carrots, beets, and radishes are root vegetables. They grow underground. They are popular with people all over the world.

**onion**

**potatoes**

**celery**

**carrots**

**radishes**

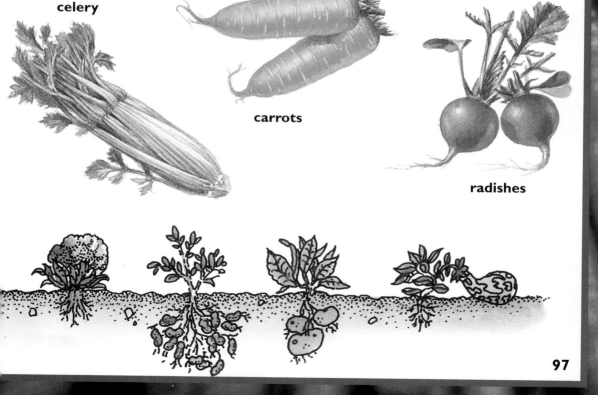

# Choose Your Plants!

**S**uppose you had an empty bowl and lots of colorful plant foods to choose from. You could make a beautiful salad!

## What To Do:

**1.** First, across the top of a piece of paper, write Seeds, Roots, Stems, Fruits, Leaves, and Flowers. Add lines to make a chart like the one shown below.

**2.** Look at the pictures of food on the opposite page. For your salad, choose 3 leaf vegetables, 2 fruits, 2 seeds, 2 stems, 2 flowers, and 2 roots.

**3.** After you write down your choices for your salad, turn to page 101 to see if you were correct. Some of the answers may surprise you!

### You Will Need:

a piece of paper

a pen or pencil

| Seeds | Roots | Stems | Fruits | Leaves | Flowers |
|-------|-------|-------|--------|--------|---------|
|       |       |       |        |        |         |
|       |       |       |        |        |         |
|       |       |       |        |        |         |

arugula

water chestnuts

tomato

broccoli

radish

cauliflower

spinach

zucchini

onions

sesame

beet

nasturium

cucumber

carrot

lettuce

sunflower

jicama

parsley

celery

bell peppers

cabbage

green peas

olives

bamboo shoots

Now, go ahead and make the salad you've planned. Put all your plant foods in a bowl, drizzle on salad dressing, and mix your salad. Yum!

**Answers:**

**seeds—**
sesame,
sunflower,
green peas;

**roots—**
radish, beet,
carrot, jicama;

**stems—**
celery, water
chestnuts,
bamboo shoots;

**fruits—**
tomato,
cucumber,
bell peppers,
olives, zucchini;

**leaves—**
onions, parsley,
lettuce, cabbage,
arugula;

**flowers—**
broccoli,
cauliflower,
nasturtium.

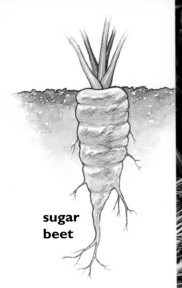

sugar
beet

A worker harvests sugar cane. After all the sugar has been squeezed out, the woody stems of sugar cane can be used to make plastics, fuel, cattle feed, and building materials.

# Flavorings from Plants

**W**ithout plants, life wouldn't be as tasty. Why? Because many of the flavors, spices, and sweeteners that make food taste good come from plants.

Sugar comes mainly from two plants, sugar beets and sugar cane. Sugar beets grow in most parts of Europe where the climate is quite mild. They are shaped like fat, white carrots. Sugar beets are shredded

**peppermint**

and cooked in water. The sweet liquid that results is made into sugar.

Maple syrup comes from sugar maple trees, which grow in North America. The sweetness is in the juice, or sap, of the trees. When holes are drilled in the tree, the sap flows out.

Nearly all the spices that make your tongue tingle also come from plants. Peppermint flavor comes from an oil made from the leaves of the peppermint plant. Pepper is the dried, ground-up berries of a shrub. Cinnamon is the bark of a tree. Mustard is made from the ground-up seeds of the mustard plant, a little **herb** with yellow flowers.

Honey comes from plants, too. Bees make it from **nectar** they collect from flowers.

People keep bees in hives like this one. They collect the honey the bees make.

**Brazil nut**

**cashews**

**walnut**

**kola nut**

**pecan**

**peach**

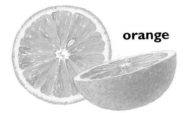

**orange**

**grapes**

# Plants for a Party

It's party time! The table is piled high with drinks and sweets, and all of them have come from plants.

Want some juice? Just about any fruit can be squeezed to make juice. Apricots, peaches, oranges, apples, grapes, guava, and passion fruit, even lemons—all these make delicious drinks. How about a fizzy soda? Cola is flavored with kola nuts, which grow on a tropical tree.

Chocolate is made with beans from the cacao tree, which grows mainly in Africa. Coconut is the "meat" of the hard-shelled seeds of the coconut palm. Licorice comes from the dried root of the licorice plant. Vanilla comes from the fruit of the vanilla orchid.

# Make Crunchies

Here's a tasty treat to serve at a party. Have a grown-up help you use the stove!

## You Will Need:

2 cups breakfast cereal (cornflakes or crisped rice)

2 tablespoons butter

2 teaspoons corn syrup

3 tablespoons cocoa powder

3 tablespoons powdered sugar

a wooden spoon

a saucepan

paper muffin cups

## What To Do:

**1.** Ask a grown-up to help you gently melt the butter and corn syrup in a saucepan over low heat. Mix well.

**2.** Turn off the heat. Add the cocoa powder and powdered sugar. Mix well. Then gently stir in the cereal.

**3.** Fill the muffin cups with the mixture and allow them to cool for 30 minutes. Serve your chocolate crunchies with a glass of milk or water!

In the African bush, or countryside, some villagers build their huts from plant stems.

# Building with Plants

**I**t makes good sense to use local materials when you're building a house. People who live near a forest use wood from the trees growing there. The skillful people with **bamboo** nearby use bamboo for many building jobs.

Bamboo is really a kind of grass. It grows up to 120 feet (37 meters) high, with a trunk 12 inches (30 centimeters) across. Many farmers in Asia live in bamboo houses and keep their chickens and pigs in bamboo cages. They water their crops with pipes made from hollow bamboo stalks.

Bamboo also helps people make buildings. Strong bamboo rods make excellent lightweight platforms for workers to stand on. Bamboo rods covered in concrete make a sturdy framework for buildings.

Water plants called rushes and reeds are also very important building materials in the areas where they grow. The marsh Arabs, or Ma'dan, of Iraq use reeds to build their houses.

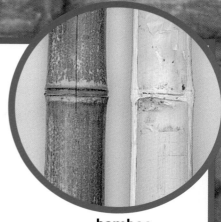

**bamboo**

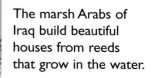

The marsh Arabs of Iraq build beautiful houses from reeds that grow in the water.

# Plants for Wearing

**cotton sweatshirt**

**cotton plant**

Plants give us many of the products used to make clothing. Your favorite old sweatshirt may be made from soft cotton. The strong, waterproof soles of your shoes are probably made of rubber.

Cotton comes from the seed pods of a plant. When the pods are ripe, they look like fluffy balls. The fluff can be twisted into thread and then woven into cloth.

Flax and hemp plants have stringy **fibers** (FY buhrz) in their stalks. The stalks are dried and scraped, then combed into long strips that can be spun into thread. Flax fibers are woven into a fine cloth called linen. Hemp makes coarser material that is used to make carpets and rope.

Rubber trees are often grown in large forests called plantations. To get the rubber out of a tree, workers make slanting cuts in the bark. Juice called latex (LAY tehks) oozes out of the cuts and drips into a container underneath. The latex is taken to a factory and made into rubber.

Latex oozes from a rubber tree, *above*. This juice is used to make things like the rubber bottom of a gym shoe.

# Wood and Paper

**T**he forests of the world give us wood. Wood is part of many products. The strong, beautiful wood of such trees as beech, oak, mahogany, teak, and walnut is used in building and to make fine furniture, musical instruments, and woodcarvings. Wood from pine, spruce, and cedar also are used in building and in making furniture, and to make pencils.

Much of the wood harvested in the world is used to make paper. Without paper, we'd have no books, no cardboard, and no newspapers. Most paper is made from wood pulp. It takes the timber of thousands of trees to make the paper for just one edition of a large daily newspaper.

Wise foresters are careful to plant trees to replace those they cut down, but it's important that people reuse and recycle as much paper as they can. Saving our waste paper could save a tree from the ax!

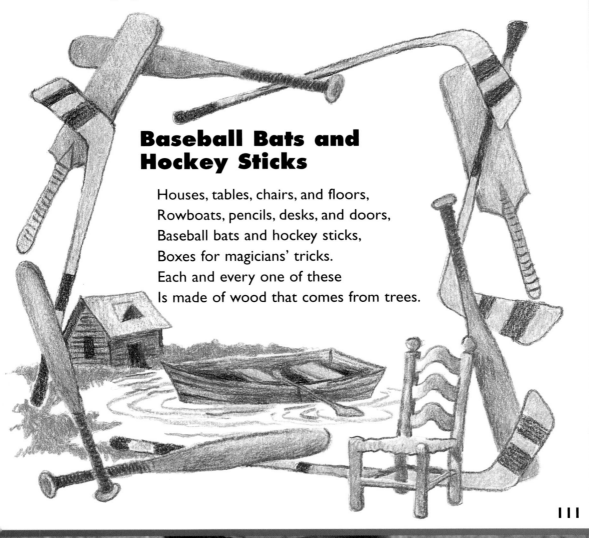

## Baseball Bats and Hockey Sticks

Houses, tables, chairs, and floors,
Rowboats, pencils, desks, and doors,
Baseball bats and hockey sticks,
Boxes for magicians' tricks.
Each and every one of these
Is made of wood that comes from trees.

# Oxygen!

**D**id you know that every green plant is like a kind of factory? Each one makes food sunrise to sunset. As it produces food, it gives off an invisible gas called **oxygen** (AHK suh juhn).

Oxygen is a very important gas. People and animals must have oxygen to live. People and animals take in oxygen when they breathe. You might think that all the oxygen would soon be used up. It would be, if we didn't have green plants! All day long, they put oxygen into the air.

People and animals give something back to plants, too. People and animals breathe out **carbon dioxide** (KAR buhn dy AHK syd). Plants need this gas to make food for themselves.

Plants use the carbon dioxide that people and animals breathe out. They give off oxygen that people and animals breathe in.

oxygen

carbon dioxide

# Watch a Plant Make Oxygen

You can watch a plant make oxygen.

## What To Do:

**1.** If you don't have a funnel, ask a grown-up to make one by cutting the top off a 1-liter drink bottle.

**2.** Lay the jar or bowl in the sink along with the funnel and bottle. Fill the sink with cool water deep enough to cover them and fill them completely.

**3.** Put an elodea plant in the jar or bowl. While they are still underwater, slide the wide end of the funnel into the jar or bowl and over the plant. Slide the tube or bottle over the funnel.

**4.** Stand the jar or bowl upright with the plant, funnel, and small bottle in it, as shown. The bottle should be filled to the top with water. Put the bowl in a sunny spot.

After a few hours, the space at the top of the tube will be filled with bubbles. It may even have a big air space in it. What happened? The elodea plant has been making oxygen all day. The oxygen has pushed some of the water out of the tube.

## You Will Need:

an elodea plant (you can find this at pet stores that sell aquarium supplies)

a wide jar or glass bowl

water

a clear funnel or 1-liter plastic drink bottle

a clear small bottle

# Plants Give Energy

**A**ll animals need green plants to survive, even if they don't eat plants.

Plants use sunlight, water, and air to grow and store up energy. When animals eat plants, they get energy from them. When a cow eats grass, for example, it

When you eat meat or eggs or drink milk from animals, you get energy from the plants that the animals ate.

takes in energy stored in the grass. It uses some of this energy to grow—to make bones and meat. It also uses some of this energy to make milk. Chickens eat plant food, too. They use the energy to grow and to produce eggs.

When you drink milk from a cow or eat eggs from a chicken, you are getting some of this plant energy into your body. Some people who do not eat meat get all their energy straight from plants.

# Plants for Health

**F**or thousands of years, people have used plants to make mild medicines and germ-killers. The juice of the aloe plant helps heal burns.

Long ago, people bought herbal medicines from herb sellers like this one.

116

Aspirin is made from a chemical from the bark of the willow tree.

**ASPIRIN**

From coast to coast, over 80 million taken daily!

- Lowers fever
- Relieves pain
- Reduces swelling

Leeks not only make a tasty soup, but also a soothing rub for insect stings.

Plants are used to make powerful medicines, too. These medicines are made in laboratories, and people get them from a doctor. The leaves of the foxglove, with its tall, pretty flowers, is used to make digitalis (dihj uh TAL ihs). This medicine helps certain kinds of heart problems. Quinine (KWY nyn), a medicine made from the bark of the cinchona (sihn KOH nuh) tree, helps bring down high fevers. There is one thing you should remember about these plants. They are all poisonous. If you ate one of them, you might die. But when these plants are used in medicines, they help people get well.

The juice of the aloe plant, *below*, helps heal burns.

Foxglove, *left*, is used to make a medicine.

# Plants for Beauty

**F**lowers are not the only beautiful things we get from plants. Plants are used for musical instruments, perfumes, dyes, and even jewelry.

The violins and clarinets in big orchestras as well as the guitars of folk and rock musicians are made of wood that comes from trees. Many Asian musical instruments are made of

This man is playing a bamboo flute in Indonesia.

bamboo, including a Japanese horn called a shaku hachi, a Chinese flute called a xiao, and a Balinese xylophone called a fungklih.

Many lovely perfumes are made of oil from flowers. People also can use the juice of flowers, berries, and bark to add color to cloth. Today, most colors are made from coal tar. Coal-tar dyes also come from plants, because coal comes from trees that died long ago.

Sweet-smelling jasmine flowers are used to make fine perfume.

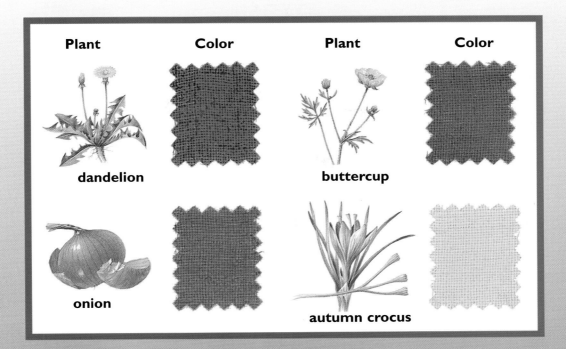

| Plant | Color | Plant | Color |
|-------|-------|-------|-------|
| dandelion | | buttercup | |
| onion | | autumn crocus | |

Necklaces and other jewelry are also often made of a yellowish rock called amber. Amber started out as a sticky gum that oozed from ancient evergreen trees. Over millions of years, this gum turned hard as rock.

amber jewelry

# Jobs For Plant Lovers

**D**o you ever wonder exactly how plants live and grow? Have you ever taken a flower apart to see what was inside it? If so, maybe some day you'll want to work with plants.

**Botanists** (BAHT uh nihsts) study plants. They look at the features of plants and where and how plants grow.

Botanists may study plants in their natural environment, such as in the water, *below,* or in the desert, *above.* Or they may work in a laboratory, *top right.*

**Chemists** (KEHM ihsts) often study ways to make new products from plants. They are the people who have invented things like cellophane (SEHL uh fayn), a clear, smooth wrapping for food. Margarine, face creams, and many other useful products also are made from plants.

An agronomist tests soils to see which are best for these plants.

**Agronomists** (uh GRAHN uh mihsts) are scientists who help farmers raise food to feed people around the world. They discover ways to make plants grow larger and healthier. They study the soil to help it grow more things.

**Gardeners, landscape architects,** and other workers plant and care for the flowers and trees you see in parks, zoos, wildlife reserves, and gardens. Gardeners and landscapers also work for towns and cities. They plant and care for the trees, bushes, and beds of flowers along streets and around many public buildings. Some gardeners grow plants and bulbs for sale. People buy them for their own homes and gardens.

This gardener is trimming plants.

**A florist** is a gardener and an artist combined. Florists grow and sell plants and flowers. They also make the beautiful bouquets you see on special occasions.

A florist makes beautiful flower arrangements.

**Photographers and artists** can work with plants, too. Pictures of plants are often used in magazines, calendars, and books. And specially trained artists can paint pictures of plants that look as real as photographs.

This photographer specializes in taking pictures of plants.

lilac

# How Does Your Garden Grow?

seed

**O**utside, gardens may be small patches or very big orchards. Vegetables and berries grow ripe and juicy. Flowers bloom in amazing colors. They brighten window boxes and lure butterflies to pots on porches, decks, and balconies.

Start a garden inside and you have even more nature to enjoy. Potted greens are bright and lovely. Herbs offer smell and taste sensations, and when dried, last even longer. Terrariums can hold what look like tiny jungles.

Be a gardener. Start with the gardening tips on the following pages.

tulip

coleus

These plants grow well on a window sill.

geranium      chives      ivy

# Indoor Gardens

**W**ould you like to have an indoor garden of your very own? One way to do it is to buy house plants. Philodendrons, sanseveria, jades, and rubber plants, which grow wild in tropical areas, make good house plants. These plants don't need much light—just a warm room, a little water, and a dusting now and then.

You can put house plants on a window sill or table near plenty of sunlight. Keep the soil damp, but not muddy. Flower pots have holes in them to let water seep out, so put a dish under each pot to catch the water. If your plants grow bigger, you can move them to bigger pots!

You can grow plants in clean tin cans or cottage-cheese cartons. Ask a grown-up to put a few small holes in the bottom of these homemade pots. Plants such as ivy or philodendrons look great in glass bowls. But a glass bowl must have a little gravel at the bottom to catch the water that seeps out of the dirt.

**TRY THIS!**

**1** Instead of buying plants, try asking a friend or neighbor for a cutting. A cutting is a stem or branch cut from another plant. Taking a cutting doesn't harm the plant. Just stick the stem in a cup of water in the sun until it grows roots. Then plant it in soil.

These plants also grow well indoors.

**coleus**     **cactus**

# Gardens in Glass

moneywort

**A** terrarium is an indoor garden in a glass container. In the 1830's, an English doctor named Nathaniel Ward became the first person to study how plants live in terrariums. He invented a glass-and-wood box that was used to keep plants alive on long ocean journeys. For many years terrariums were called Wardian cases, after Dr. Ward. Make your own terrarium. It's like having a tiny forest all to yourself.

club moss

## You Will Need:

a glass box, bowl,
    or jar, with a lid
    or plastic wrap

pebbles

potting soil

charcoal

water

small plants

hepatica

## What To Do:

**1.** Put a layer of pebbles in the bottom for water to drain into. Cover the pebbles with a layer of broken charcoal for added drainage. Place potting soil on top of that. Water the soil until it is damp, but not muddy.

**2.** Choose your plants. The best kinds of plants for closed terrariums are plants that like damp conditions, such as ferns, baby's tears, African violets, mosses, or very small evergreens. Arrange the plants so that your terrarium looks like a tiny forest. Remember, leave room for them to grow.

**3.** Keep your terrarium in a place that is bright but not sunny. If you cover your terrarium, the temperature and moisture should stay in balance. If the glass gets too moist, remove the lid for a short time.

You can plant a pretty terrarium in a big bottle.

# Outdoor Gardens

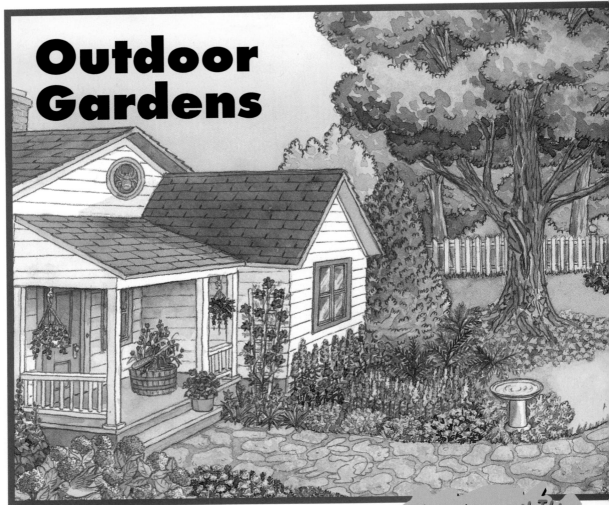

**P**lanting an outdoor garden is great fun! It's a real thrill to watch little green sprouts come poking up from the places where you planted seeds.

What kind of garden do you want? A garden full of crunchy, delicious vegetables? Or a flower garden with colors and scents to delight you? All you need for an outdoor garden is a small

**TRY THIS!**
**1**

An outdoor garden can become a fine home for animals as well as plants. Can you find 10 animals hidden in the garden above? *See answers on page 133.*

patch of earth. Ask an adult to help you find a good spot.

Most gardens do best in sunny spots. Plants that love sunshine include yuccas, geraniums, and yarrows. If you live where it's hot and dry for much of the year, you can grow euphorbias and cactuses.

But you can also plant a garden in a shady spot. You just have to choose plants that like shade. Hostas, impatiens, begonias, and ferns all are shade-loving plants.

You can buy seeds or bulbs for all kinds of plants. If the seeds are very tiny, you can plant them on a tray of soil indoors. Cover them lightly with soil and water them. Keep them in a warm

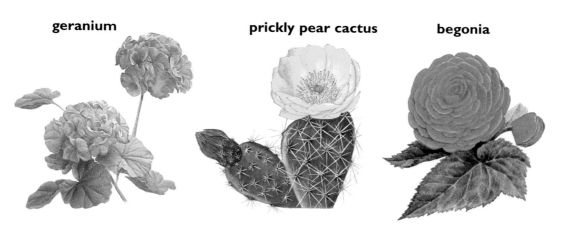

| geranium | prickly pear cactus | begonia |

place but out of direct
sunlight. The small plants
can be planted outside when
they are big enough for
you to handle.

To give your garden the best
possible start, you have to prepare
the ground first. Pull up all the
**weeds.** Weeds are any plants
that are not wanted in your
garden. Then dig and rake the
ground to loosen the soil. Mark off
rows for the seeds or plants. To make
holes for seeds, push a pointed stick
into the ground. To put in small plants,
you'll need a trowel. Use it like a big
spoon to scoop out holes. Gently
cover the seeds or roots with soil.

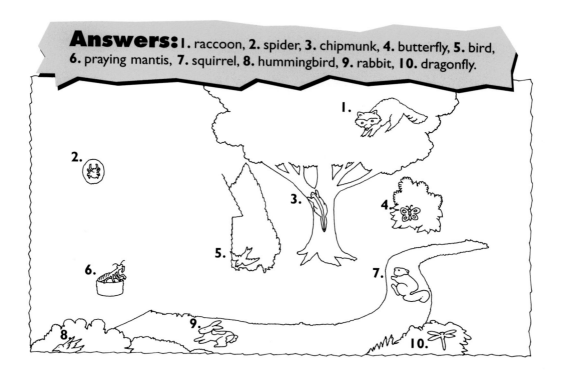

Water the garden until the soil is damp but not muddy. The best time to water is in the evening or early morning. That way, the sun won't dry up the water before it soaks into the dirt.

By early summer, garden plants are usually growing well, but so are the weeds! You can either pull up weeds by hand, or gently scrape small weeds from the ground with a hoe.

When it's time to harvest, your garden will reward you for all your hard work. Colorful flowers look pretty in a vase. And tasty fruits and vegetables are a hit at mealtime!

# Grow Your Own Sunflowers

**N**ative Americans once used powdered sunflower seeds to make bread and to thicken soup. Today, people still enjoy eating sunflower treats. Here's how to grow your own sunflowers.

## You Will Need:

several sunflower seeds in their shells

a large, sunny patch of soil

water

several stakes

ties

## What To Do:

**1.** Plant the seeds about 1 inch (2.5 centimeters) deep.

**2.** Water the ground every day. Shoots will appear in 10 to 14 days.

**3.** When the plants are about 4 inches (10 centimeters) tall, move them so they are about 3 feet (60 centimeters) apart.

**4.** These plants will grow very fast. They can grow up to 10 feet (3 meters) tall, with flowers as big as dinner plates! Tie each sunflower to a stake as it grows, to keep it standing tall.

**5.** When the flower dries up, cut off the head and rub the seeds out onto some newspaper. Shell some of the seeds and add them to salads, or roast them in the oven. Put some in a bird feeder. Store the rest in an envelope and keep them for planting next year. You may never have to buy sunflower seeds again!

# Make a Simple Potpourri

TRY THIS! 2

**P**eople make mixtures of dried fragrant plants and spices to make their homes smell nice. These mixtures are called potpourri (poh puhr EE). Use this recipe to make some for your room.

## What To Do:

**1.** In a small bowl, make a spice mixture by mixing the cloves, cinnamon, and salt.

**2.** Place the flowers and herbs in a plastic container.

**3.** Sprinkle the spice mixture over the flowers and herbs. Add the orris root, gum bezoin, or some more salt. Add an essential, or sweet-smelling, oil if you like. Mix gently.

**4.** Cover the container tightly and let it stand. Shake it every day or two to mix the ingredients well. After 2 to 4 weeks have passed, set the mixture in a pretty basket or bowl.

## You Will Need:

- a small bowl or plastic container with lid

- I tablespoon ground cloves

- I tablespoon ground cinnamon

- 2 tablespoons uniodized salt

- about 2 cups of dried fragrant flowers and herbs, such as rose, lavender, thyme, or eucalyptus (See page 137 for how to make your own)

- a small scoop of orris root, gum bezoin, or salt (from a craft store or herbal shop)

- 3 to 4 drops of essential oil (optional)

# An Herb Garden

**H**erbs make great tea, add flavor to foods, soothe aches, relieve illnesses, and smell nice. How would you like to have fresh herbs at your fingertips? You can by growing an herb garden.

If you live where it's sunny and dry, try growing borage or marjoram outside. Herbs such as chives, chervil, lemon balm, and mint grow well in shady places.

You can also grow herbs in pots, either outdoors or on window sills. Basil, savory, cilantro, and rosemary are just a few of the herbs that grow well this way.

# Dry Your Own Herbs

TRY THIS! 1

**M**any herbs are delicious when eaten fresh. But you can also dry some to use later.

## What To Do:

**1.** Use rubber bands to fasten the stems of your fresh herbs in bunches.

**2.** Tie the bunches onto hangers with kitchen twine.

**3.** Hang the hangers in a warm, dry place for about a week, or until the leaves crumble easily.

sage   thyme   mint   parsley

**4.** Store your dried herbs in jars or bottles. Label the jars so you know which herb is in each one. Ask your parents which meals you can add your dried herbs to. Share a jar with a friend!

## You Will Need:

fresh herbs, such as oregano, basil, rosemary, dill, or thyme (preferably from your garden!)

rubber bands

metal clothes hangers

kitchen twine

small jars or bottles

# An Edible Garden

**T**he ancient Greeks loved radishes so much they made gold ornaments that looked like them and offered these golden radishes to their sun god, Apollo.

Nothing tastes quite so good as radishes or other food you have grown yourself. To grow some, you will need a small patch of flat ground that gets plenty of sunshine.

Cucumbers and zucchini grow well on stakes. They will climb up a grate or trellis. Beans are good climbing plants, too.

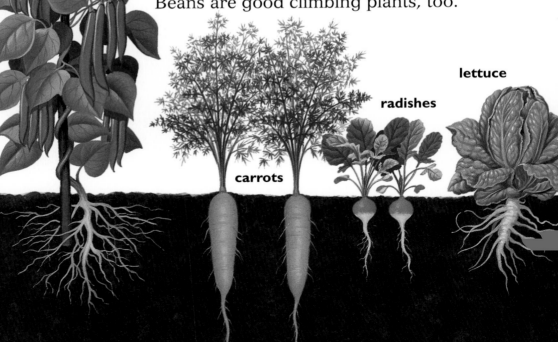

snap beans

lettuce

radishes

carrots

You can grow potatoes by cutting up a potato and planting the pieces. Make sure each piece you plant has a tiny bud, or eye, on it.

Endive, lettuce, and napa cabbage are popular leaf vegetables. Many people grow rhubarb, which will come up by itself year after year and grows well in shady spots. The plants that are beautiful as well as tasty include eggplants, sweet potatoes, and many kinds of peppers.

**tomatoes**

## TRY THIS! 2

Many people think tomatoes are vegetables. They are really the fruit of the tomato vine. You can grow some of your own. It's easy! Some varieties can be grown in a bucket. Others should be planted in the ground about 2 feet (60 cm) apart. Attach the stems to stakes for support. Keep them watered, then pick and enjoy!

**cucumbers**

# One-Year Flowers

**M**ost flowers that people plant in the spring are annuals. **Annuals** (AN yoo uhlz) are plants that live only one growing season. They sprout from seeds that are planted in the spring. In the summer, their flowers grow and make seeds. In the fall,

red salvia

marigold

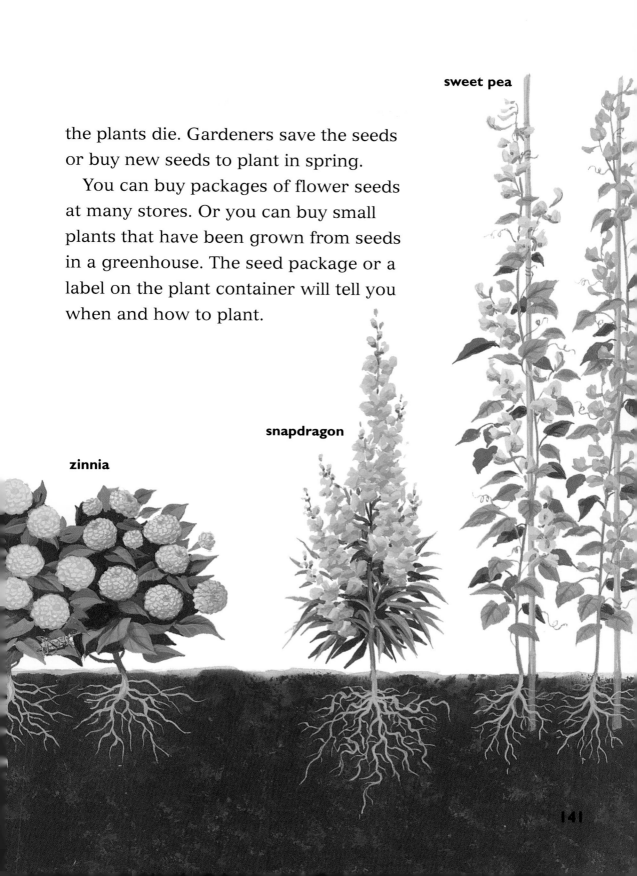

the plants die. Gardeners save the seeds or buy new seeds to plant in spring.

You can buy packages of flower seeds at many stores. Or you can buy small plants that have been grown from seeds in a greenhouse. The seed package or a label on the plant container will tell you when and how to plant.

sweet pea

snapdragon

zinnia

# Year-After-Year Flowers

**delphinium**

**S**ome flowers don't have to be planted every year. You plant them just once and leave them in the ground. From then on, they bloom each year. Tulips, for example, have beautiful cup-shaped flowers that bloom each year. Lilies have blade-shaped petals and showy stamens.

Plants that bloom every year are called **perennials.** Many perennials

**tulip**

**lily**

grow from bulbs or from bulblike parts called **corms.** Bulbs are underground buds. They are made up of a small stem covered with thick, fleshy leaves. Onions, tulips, and lilies grow from bulbs. Corms are very similar to bulbs, but their leaves are smaller and thinner. Crocuses and gladiolus grow from corms.

Most bulbs and corms should be planted in the fall. But the package they come in will tell you the best time to plant them.

Many perennials need protection during winter. The package your seeds or bulbs come in, or a gardening book, will tell you what to do for each kind.

gladiolus

chrysanthemum

crocus

# The Garden of Talking Flowers

*Through the Looking Glass,* by Lewis Carroll, tells the story of a little girl's adventures in a mysterious land. In this scene, the little girl, named Alice, meets some very special flowers.

**A**lice came upon a large flower bed with a border of daisies and a willow tree growing in the middle.

"O Tiger-lily," said Alice, addressing herself to one that was waving gracefully about in the wind. "I wish you could talk!"

"We can talk," said the Tiger-lily, "when there's anybody worth talking to."

Alice was so astonished that she could not speak for a minute. It quite seemed to take her breath away. At length, as the Tiger-lily only went on waving about, she

spoke again, in a timid voice—almost in a whisper. "And can all the flowers talk?"

"As well as you can," said the Tiger-lily. "And a great deal louder."

"It isn't manners for us to begin, you know," said the Rose, "and I really was wondering when you'd speak! Said I to myself, 'Her face has got some sense in it, though it's not a clever one!'"

Then Tiger-lily remarked,
"If only her petals curled
up a little more, she'd be all right."
Alice didn't like being criticized, so
she began asking questions. "Aren't
you sometimes frightened at being
planted out here with nobody to take
care of you?"

"There's the tree in the middle," said
the Rose. "What else is it good for?"

"But what could it do, if any danger
came?"

"It says, 'Bough-wough!' " cried a
Daisy. "That's why its branches are
called boughs!"

"Didn't you know that?" cried another Daisy, and here they all began shouting together, till the air seemed quite full of little shrill voices. "Silence, every one of you!" cried the Tiger-lily, waving itself passionately from side to side and trembling with excitement. "They know I can't get at them!" it panted, bending its quivering head towards Alice, "or they wouldn't dare to do it!"

"Never mind!" Alice said in a soothing tone and stooping down at the Daisies, who were just beginning again, she whispered, "If you don't hold your tongues, I'll pick you!"

There was silence in a moment, and several of the pink daisies turned white.

"That's right!" said the Tiger-lily. "The daisies are worst of all. When one speaks, they all begin together, and it's enough to make one wither to hear the way they go on!"

"How is it you can all talk so nicely?"
Alice said, hoping to get it into a better
temper by a compliment. "I've been in
many gardens before, but none of the
flowers could talk."

"Put your hand down and feel the
ground," said the Tiger-lily. "Then you'll
know why."

Alice did so. "It's very hard," she said,
"but I don't see what that has to do with it."

"In most gardens," the Tiger-lily said,
"they make the beds too soft—so that the
flowers are always asleep."

This sounded like a very good reason,
and Alice was quite pleased to know it.

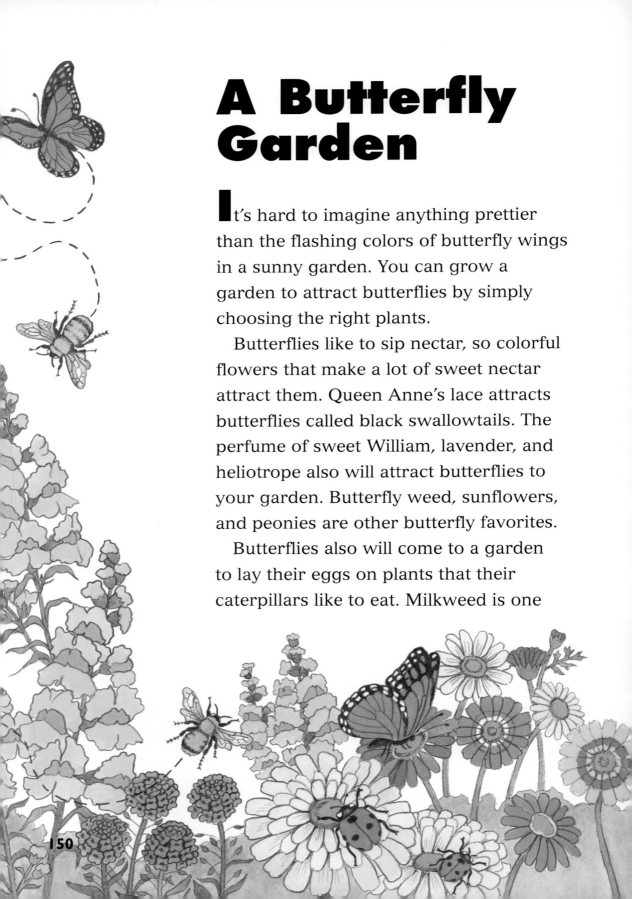

# A Butterfly Garden

It's hard to imagine anything prettier than the flashing colors of butterfly wings in a sunny garden. You can grow a garden to attract butterflies by simply choosing the right plants.

Butterflies like to sip nectar, so colorful flowers that make a lot of sweet nectar attract them. Queen Anne's lace attracts butterflies called black swallowtails. The perfume of sweet William, lavender, and heliotrope also will attract butterflies to your garden. Butterfly weed, sunflowers, and peonies are other butterfly favorites.

Butterflies also will come to a garden to lay their eggs on plants that their caterpillars like to eat. Milkweed is one of these plants. The caterpillar of the monarch butterfly eats milkweed. The caterpillar of the black swallowtail butterfly eats parsley. Several types of caterpillars feed on nettles and clover.

To welcome butterflies, you can put out large flat rocks for them to "sunbathe" on. You might also provide puddles of water where they can drink.

A caterpillar is a larva on its way to being a butterfly. Caterpillars hatch from eggs that are laid by butterflies. They eat leaves and grow. After a time, they turn into butterflies.

Butterflies and their caterpillars will visit a garden full of fragrant flowers.

Small, brightly colored flowers are perfect for a rock garden.

# A Rock Garden

If your yard has a sunny place that slopes a little, like a small hill, you can make a rock garden. It should look like a tiny bit of mountainside, where small, bright flowers grow among the rocks.

First, bring rocks to the slope. Scoop out shallow holes for them. Put the biggest rocks at the bottom. Put the smaller stones higher up on the slope. Place some of them close together and some farther apart. At least half of each rock should be buried in the dirt.

This rock garden looks like a colorful bit of mountainside.

Your rock garden won't be as big as this one. But it can be just as pretty if you work hard at it.

Finally, plant small ferns and flowering plants between the rocks. Use plants that won't grow more than 12 inches (30 centimeters) high.

Rocks in a garden can make perfect hooks for ferns to grow in.

In the past, people had their bathrooms in small buildings called outhouses. Many people planted sweet-smelling lilacs next to their outhouses to make the air around them smell better.

# A Scent Garden

**O**ne of the most wonderful things about plants is the way some of them smell. Lovely scents come from their flowers or their leaves.

The rose is a sweet-smelling favorite around the world. The sweet pea is a fragrant climbing plant. The tiny, white, bell-shaped lily of the valley has a strong perfume. Many people think that

heliotrope smells like vanilla, apple, or cherry pie. One kind of cosmos smells like chocolate.

Fragrant flowering shrubs include the winter jasmine and the gardenia. The leaves of the myrtle plant have a spicy smell when crushed. Daphne and lilacs are also favorites.

Roses fill the air with their lovely scent.

Japanese garden

# World of Gardens

In every part of the world, people have a favorite kind of garden. In a formal garden, flowers are arranged in squares, circles, or fancy shapes. Bushes are often trimmed to points, squares, or balls. Garden paths are long and straight. In Japan, many gardens have little bridges in them. In India, gardens often have ponds filled with water lilies. Gardens in Hawaii may have many ferns. Gardeners in other parts of the world often copy these favorite gardens.

These elephants won't stampede! They are evergreen trees cut and grown in the shape of elephants. This garden is in Thailand.

In a maze garden, tall shrubs are planted and trimmed to create confusing pathways. People are enjoying trying to find their way out of this English maze garden.

# Taking Care of Forests

**F**orests, just like gardens, need care if they are to stay strong and healthy. People who take care of forests are called **foresters.** There are different kinds of foresters. Some foresters work for a government. They take care of national parks and forests so that people will have places for camping, sightseeing, hunting, and fishing.

Other foresters work in woods that are owned by lumber and paper companies. They raise and care for the trees that are used to make houses, furniture, and paper.

This forester is caring for trays of seedlings in a tree nursery. Soon the seedlings will be replanted to make a new forest.

A nursery worker in Indonesia cares for tiny trees.

All foresters protect trees from insects, animals, fires, and diseases. They make sure that unhealthy trees are replaced with young, healthy ones, and that the young trees grow up to be big, healthy trees. Foresters also plant new trees to replace trees that have been cut down.

A brand-new piece of forest has been planted on the banks of a river in India.

# Names of Flowers

**D**id you ever wonder how some wildflowers got their names?

The daisy looks a little bit like an eye. And, like an eye, it opens up at the start of each day. So, long ago in England, people named it "day's eye." In time, the name became *daisy*.

**daisy**

**KNOW It All!** People have used flowers to share their feelings with one another for many years. For example, sending red roses is a way to say, "I love you." Lilies of the valley send the message that happiness is returning. Buttercups stand for riches. And when friends want to say "thank you," they may send camellias.

**lily of the valley**

The buttercup got its name because it looks like a tiny cup made of yellow butter. Long ago, people believed that butter was yellow because cows ate buttercups. But that's not true. Butter does get its color from what cows eat, but cows don't eat buttercups.

KNOW It All!! The scientific name for the buttercup family, *ranunculus*, means "little frog" in Latin. An ancient Roman scientist named Pliny the Elder gave these flowers this name because he found them living in wet places, just like frogs!

**buttercup**

Milkweed gets its name from the white juice that oozes from the stems when the plant is cut. The juice looks like milk. When the juice dries in the sun, it covers the cut like a rubbery bandage.

**milkweed**

For years, people in different parts of the world have eaten the young, spring leaves of dandelions. They thought the jagged edges of the leaf looked like a row of teeth. So, long ago, the people of France gave the plant the name *dent de lion,* which means "lion's tooth." To the people of England, *dent de lion* sounded like *dandelion,* and that's what they called the plant!

There was a pretty dandelion
With lovely, fluffy hair,
That glistened in the sunshine
And in the summer air.
But oh! this pretty dandelion
Soon grew old and gray;
And, sad to tell! her charming hair
Blew many miles away.

**dandelion**

**catnip**

One plant that many cats love is called catnip! A cat that finds a clump of catnip may roll happily around among the leaves. Many cat owners give their pets balls or toys stuffed with dried catnip leaves.

Some people like catnip too, but not usually to roll around in. They drink it. They make catnip tea by putting dried catnip leaves into boiling water and adding a little honey.

building a
road in the
jungle

# Plants Need Help, Too

**P**lants can get sick, just as people can. Insects and other animals can chew plants until they die. Fire can turn them into a pile of ashes. Polluted air from cars and factories can choke the life out of plants. And when ground is dug up for new factories, houses, and parking lots, plants lose the space they need to live.

Everyone depends on plants for beauty, food, and fresh air. So everyone needs to save them and care for them.

**orchid**

# Plants in Danger

**E**ndangered (ehn DAYN juhrd) plants need people's help to survive. A species, or kind, of plant is endangered when it is seriously close to disappearing, or becoming extinct. Scientists think as many as 20,000 different kinds of plants are endangered.

Rafflesia (ruh FLEE zhuh) is one of the world's most endangered plants because the rain forests in which it lives are being destroyed. The giant rafflesia has the largest flower in the world. It grows up to 3 feet (91 centimeters) wide, and it smells like rotten meat! The smell attracts the flies that pollinate the flower.

For many years, scientists believed that the Virginia round-leaf birch and a type of Australian elaeocarpus tree were extinct. Then, in 1975, a scientist found a group of round-leaf birches alive and well. Since then, people have worked to protect the round-leaf birch.

In 1992, scientists discovered that elaeocarpus trees were still alive, too, growing in the rain forest of New South Wales. They have found more than 100 elaeocarpus trees in the wild since then.

A rafflesia plant is all flower and no leaves. The huge flower has a strong smell that flies like.

# Threats from Animals

**A**ll over the world, plants are being destroyed by animals. Sometimes this is perfectly natural and is part of the balance of nature. Other times, it can be disastrous.

Insects such as caterpillars and grubs, which later become beetles, often eat leaves or burrow into the wood of trees. But sometimes, a nest of tent caterpillars eats all the buds or young leaves on a tree. When this happens, the tree will die.

Big problems also arise when people bring animals to areas where they don't belong. Rabbits have destroyed valuable grazing land in Australia. They eat the grasses ranchers need for their livestock. Rabbits were

Beavers cut down trees for food and shelter. A large beaver family may damage many trees near the lake or river where it lives.

tent caterpillars munching leaves

turned loose in 1859 by British settlers. But in Australia, rabbits have few natural enemies, so now there are too many rabbits.

In Hawaii, escaped pigs and goats have destroyed many rare plants. They trample the plants and eat the roots so the plants can't grow back. Goats also may eat all the plants on a hillside. With no roots to hold the soil, rain can wash it down the hill. This loss of soil is called **erosion** (ih ROH zhuhn) and keeps plants from growing. Today, about half of Hawaii's plants are either very rare, endangered, or already extinct.

These goats have caused erosion on a hillside in Hawaii by eating all the plants.

# Threats from People

**P**eople are a plant's worst enemies. This is mainly because people want or need things that can be made from plants.

Many kinds of plants are becoming rare because of their beauty. People often dig these plants up and take them home. The beautiful flowers of orchids and some cactuses have made them targets for collectors. The hedgehog and Knowlton cactuses of the American Southwest are now endangered.

The beautiful flowers of orchids make them tempting to pick. Many kinds of orchids throughout the world are now endangered.

Great numbers of palm trees are destroyed for their stems, which are made into furniture, and for their fruit. Hundreds of types of palms are endangered today.

People kill many plants for use in medicines. The Pacific yew was once the source of a drug that doctors use to treat cancer. But getting the drug threatened these trees so much that researchers found other ways of making the drug.

People kill plants when they develop land. Lots of land is used for building. Even more is changed into farmland or

grazing land for cattle and other animals. As the population increases, people build more roads, houses, factories, mines, shopping centers, and parking lots.

But plants need their own special place to live in, too. They need the right kind of soil, the right temperature, and the right amount of rainfall. They need the right **habitat** (HAB uh tat). When habitats disappear, the animals that live there often disappear too. If we destroy too many natural habitats, we may lose many of the plants and animals in our lives.

When people clear land for farming or building, habitats are lost. Little by little, the great forests, rich wetlands, and rolling prairies are disappearing. If this continues, the beauty of these natural things will be gone forever.

# Vanishing Tropical Rain Forests

Everywhere in the world people are taking over more land. In tropical rain forests, parts of the forest are cut down and burned to make room for crops. After a time, the soil in these parts is no longer good for growing crops. Then the people move on to another place. It is hard for new plants to grow in the poor soil. Without plants and trees, the soil that is left washes away.

People also destroy tropical rain forests to get lumber. The trees that grow in these forests provide valuable wood. Every day, in many countries, people are cutting down trees that have taken years and years to grow.

In the world's biggest tropical rain forest, the Amazon rain forest in South America, people are building a highway. Trees are being cut down to build the highway. When the road is finished, more people will travel into the rain forest. This may lead to even more destruction.

The world's tropical rain forests are home to many kinds of rare animals. They may have lived there for many thousands of years in the safety of the trees. But now the tropical rain forest is disappearing fast. Scientists believe that some rain forest animals will die out even before they have been discovered!

Heavy machinery cuts down trees in the rain forest of Brazil. Workers in this picture are building the Trans-Amazon Highway.

# The Enemy in the Air

Imagine a world in which most of the trees are dead, where leaves and flowers are spotted with disease, and fruits can't grow. It wouldn't be a very nice world. But many scientists fear that's what our world may be like someday—if we don't do something now about air pollution.

Air pollution begins when gases from automobiles, factories, lawn mowers, and burning wood enter the air. **Acid rain** forms when certain chemicals from air pollution rise up and mix with the water in the clouds.

This pine tree was killed by air pollution from cars and trucks.

The rain or snow that falls from these polluted clouds hurts the leaves of trees. The trees slowly lose their leaves and die. Acid rain also soaks into the soil and damages plants and crops. Many of the world's forests—especially the pine forests of northern Europe—are suffering from the effects of acid rain.

Fumes from cars and trucks have damaged these leaves from an aspen tree.

Air pollution is a very serious problem. But scientists and many other people are working on it. They're trying to clean up the air and keep it clean, for the sake of people and plants.

# Fire!

The forest rangers are worried. The weather is hot and there has been no rain for a long time. They know the forest is as dry as dust. It would take only a tiny spark or a lightning strike to turn the whole forest into a roaring, raging sea of fire.

Firefighters on the ground battle flames with streams of water. Airplane crews drop water or chemicals from above to help put out the blaze. They are all trying to save the forest.

From their watchtower high above the trees, the rangers see a thin spiral of smoke. Fire! There's a fire in the forest!

A quick call for help goes out. Firefighters rush to the blaze in trucks. Working quickly, they battle the blaze with streams of water and shovelfuls of soil. They chop down trees and dig up the ground to keep the fire from spreading.

A dry forest can burn quickly.

Overhead, airplanes swoop over the fire, dropping water and chemicals on it. Other planes bring firefighters called smoke jumpers. They parachute into places that the firefighters on the ground can't reach.

At last, after many hours or sometimes many days, the fire is out. Thousands of trees have been saved. Thousands of trees have been destroyed.

The wood of the ombu tree of Argentina is so moist that it will not burn. It can survive not only fires, but also insect attacks, drought, and violent storms.

KNOW It All!

This rare welwitschia plant in Namibia is protected by a fence.

# What's Being Done?

**P**eople are working together in many ways to save the world's plants.

Some people work directly with plants. Growers trade seeds with one another to help a species' chances to survive. They also grow endangered plants in greenhouses. Then they replant the plants in the wild. Sometimes, people build fences around rare plants in the wild to keep away animals that may eat or trample them.

Two important groups that work to protect plants are the International Union

for the Conservation of Nature and Natural Resources (IUCN) and the World Wildlife Fund (WWF). They inform people about endangered plants and raise money to help save them.

Many governments have passed laws to protect plants. In the United States, the Endangered Species Act was passed in 1973. This law protects endangered plants and animals from hunting, collecting, and other activities that could harm them or their communities. Many countries also have signed an agreement called CITES. By signing this agreement, they promise not to buy or sell endangered plants or animals, or products made from them.

# You Can Help

**Y**ou may think there is not much you can do to help save plants. But there are lots of things you can do. When you go on a hike, stay on the path. Leaving the path harms the plants.

Sometimes you can help plants by *not* doing things. Do not pick or dig up wildflowers and other plants. Even though some are still plentiful, others are becoming rare. Enjoy wildflowers by taking pictures, or by drawing them. Buy seeds

gathered in national parks or from seed companies. Then other people can enjoy the wildflowers, too.

Remind grown-ups to be very careful with campfires or outdoor cooking. Make sure that fires are out completely before you leave the area. If the weather has been very dry, don't build fires at all. And when you leave camp, take all your garbage with you to a garbage can.

Don't break off limbs or peel bark from trees. The outside bark protects a tree from harmful insects and fungus. The inner bark moves food from the leaves to the roots. Peeling off a tree's bark or breaking off its limbs can kill the tree.

You can help save trees by **recycling**. Many communities have recycling programs. This means that used paper is picked up and taken to factories that use it to make new paper. Your family can recycle junk mail, old school papers, grocery bags, cereal boxes, toilet paper tubes, and even the tags from teabags.

Stay on the path.

Take your trash home.

Enjoy wildflowers where they are. Don't pick them.

TRY THIS!
1

How does your family help cut back on air pollution? One way is to walk or ride bikes instead of using the car. Another is to not use the car, grill, lawn mower, and other polluters on pollution-alert days in your area.

182

These children are helping to save the world of plants by planting new trees on their school grounds.

183

# Glossary

Here are some of the words you read in this book. Many of them may be new to you. Some are hard to pronounce. But since you will see them again, they are good words to know. Next to each word, you will see how to say it correctly: **conservation** (KAHN suhr VAY shuhn). The part shown in small capital letters is said a little more loudly than the rest of the word. The part in large capital letters is said the loudest. Under each word are one or two sentences that tell what the word means.

## A

**acid rain** (AS ihd rayn)
Acid rain is a dangerous form of pollution. It forms when certain chemicals from air pollution rise up into the air and mix with the water in the clouds.

**agronomist** (uh GRAHN uh mihst)
An agronomist is a person who studies how to improve crops and the soil they grow in.

**algae** (AL jee)
Algae are plantlike living things without stems, roots, or leaves. They live in water or moist places and make their own food. One of these creatures is called an alga (AL guh).

**annual** (AN yoo uhl)
An annual is a plant that lives only one year.

**anther** (AN thuhr)
The anther is a tiny sack on a stem inside a flower. The anthers make pollen.

## B

**bamboo** (bam BOO)
Bamboo is a fast-growing grass with woody stems that can be used for building material.

**biennial** (by EHN ee uhl)
A biennial is a plant that lives for two years.

**boll** (bohl)
A boll is the seed pod of a cotton plant.

**botanist** (BAHT uh nihst)
A botanist is a person who studies plants.

**bulb** (buhlb)
A bulb is an underground bud.

## C

**canopy** (KAN uh pee)
The canopy of a tropical rain forest is the main "umbrella" of huge leaves.

**carbon dioxide** (KAR buhn dy AHK syd)
Carbon dioxide is the gas that plants need to make food. Animals and people breathe out carbon dioxide.

**cell** (sehl)
A cell is the smallest part of all living things.

**cellulose** (SEHL yuh lohs)
Cellulose is a tough material that forms the cell walls of plants.

**cereal** (SIHR ee uhl)
Cereal is any plant, such as wheat or oats, that produces a grain used for food.

184

**chemist** (KEHM ihst)

A chemist is a person who studies nonliving substances to find out what they are made of, how they act, and how they change.

**chlorophyll** (KLAWR uh fihl)

Chlorophyll is the green substance that plants use along with sunlight and water to make food.

**community** (kuh MYOO nuh tee)

A community is a group of plants and animals that live together.

**conifer** (KAHN uh fuhr)

A conifer is any of a large group of trees and shrubs that bear cones. Most conifers are evergreen.

**conservation** (KAHN suhr VAY shuhn)

Conservation is the protection and careful use of plants, animals, and natural resources, such as water, air, soil, and minerals.

**corm** (korm)

A corm is a small bulb from which a new plant grows.

**cycads** (SY kadz)

Cycads are tropical plants that look like palms with fernlike leaves. They are related to needleleaf trees, such as pines and spruces.

# D

**deciduous** (dih SIHJ oo uhs)

A deciduous tree is one that loses its leaves at a certain time of year and later grows new ones.

**digest** (dy JEHST)

To digest is to break down food so that it can be used by the body.

# E

**embryo** (EHM bree oh)

The embryo is the part of the seed that grows into a plant.

**emergent layer** (ih MER juhnt LAY uhr)

The emergent layer of a tropical rain forest is made up of the top branches of the tallest trees.

**endangered** (ehn DAYN juhrd)

To be endangered is to be in danger of dying out.

**erosion** (ih ROH zhun)

Erosion is when soil is worn away by water, wind, or other forces.

# F

**fiber** (FY buhr)

A fiber is a long, threadlike piece of a plant.

**forester** (FAWR uh stuhr)

A forester is a person who takes care of a forest.

**fungi** (FUHN jy)

Fungi are plantlike living things with no leaves, chlorophyll, or flowers. One of these living things is called a fungus.

# G

**germinate** (JUR muh nayt)

To germinate is to sprout.

**gingko** (GIHNG koh)

A gingko is a large tree with leaves shaped like little fans.

# H

**habitat** (HAB uh tat)

A habitat is the place where a plant or animal lives. It has the right kind of soil, the right temperature, and the right amount of rainfall to meet the plant's or animal's needs.

**herb** (urb)

An herb is a plant whose leaves or other parts are used for medicine, seasoning, food, or perfume.

# K

**kingdom** (KIHNG duhm)

A kingdom is a large group of living things that share important features.

# M

**mangrove** (MANG grohv)

A mangrove is a tree that grows in salt water.

**mineral** (MIHN uhr uhl)

A mineral is a solid substance that comes from the earth and is not animal or vegetable.

# N

**nectar** (NEHK tuhr)

Nectar is a sweet liquid made by flowers.

# O

**organism** (OR guh nihz uhm)

An organism is a living thing.

**ovule** (OH vyool)

The ovule is the part of a plant that develops into a seed.

**oxygen** (AHK suh juhn)

Oxygen is a gas without color or odor. It is part of the air we breathe.

# P

**Pampas** (PAHM puhz)

The Pampas is a grassland in South America.

**perennial** (puh REHN ee uhl)

A perennial is a plant that blooms year after year.

**pistil** (PIHS tuhl)

A pistil is the female, egg-making part of a flower.

**pollen** (PAHL uhn)

Pollen is a yellowish powder formed in the anthers of flowers. When pollen reaches a flower's ovule, a seed is usually formed.

**pollination** (PAHL uh NAY shuhn)

Pollination is carrying pollen from one flower to another.

**prairie** (PRAIR ee)

A prairie is a habitat of tall grasses.

# R

**rafflesia** (ruh FLEE zhuh)

The rafflesia is a plant that has the world's largest flower.

**recycling** (ree SY klihng)

Recycling is reusing trash, such as paper, plastic, and aluminum cans, to make new products.

**reproduce** (REE pruh DOOS)

To reproduce is to make new living things.

**runner** (RUHN uhr)

A runner is a stem that grows sideways. New plants grow on the runners and root themselves wherever they touch the ground.

# S

**savanna** (suh VAN uh)

A savanna is a grassland with a few trees and clumps of grasses.

**sow** (SOH)

To sow is to plant seeds in soil.

**species** (SPEE sheez)

A species is a group of plants or animals that are like each other in many ways.

**spore** (spawr)

A spore is a tiny, seedlike cell that comes from a living thing. Molds, fungi, and some plants, such as ferns, may grow from spores.

**stamen** (STAY muhn)

A stamen is a slender stalk inside a flower. The stamen supports the anther.

**steppe** (stehp)

A steppe is a habitat of short grasses.

**stigma** (STIHG muh)

The stigma is the part of a plant that receives the pollen.

# T

**temperate** (TEHM puhr iht)

A temperate place is one that has warm summers, cold winters, and plenty of rainfall.

**timber line** (TIHM buhr lyn)

The timber line is the highest place on a mountain where trees can grow.

**tuber** (TOO buhr)

A tuber is a thick, underground stem. New plants can grow from tubers.

**tundra** (TUHN druh)

The tundra is a great, treeless plain in a cold place, such as the Arctic.

# W

**weed** (weed)

A weed is a plant that grows where it is not wanted.

# Index

This index is an alphabetical list of important topics covered in this book. It will help you find information given in both words and pictures. To help you understand what an entry means, there is sometimes a helping word in parentheses, for example, **annual** (plant). If there is information in both words and pictures, you will see the words *with pictures* in parentheses after the page number. If there is only a picture, you will see the word *picture* in parentheses after the page number.

# Illustration Acknowledgments

The Publishers of Childcraft gratefully acknowledge the courtesy of the following illustrators, photographers, agencies, and organizations for illustrations in this volume. When all the illustrations for a sequence of pages are from a single source, the inclusive page numbers are given. Credits should be read from top to bottom, left to right, on their respective pages. All illustrations are the exclusive property of the publishers of Childcraft unless names are marked with an asterisk (*).

| | |
|---|---|
| Cover | Water lily—© Cathy Melloan*; Tree—David Webb; Tomato—Eileen Mueller Neill; Pine cones—James Teason |
| Back Cover | David Webb |
| 1 | David Webb; Eileen Mueller Neill; James Teason |
| 2-3 | C. William Randall; James Teason; James Teason |
| 4-5 | Christabel King; Mike Mogg; James Teason |
| 6-7 | Peter Geissler; Jane Pickering; David Thompson |
| 8-9 | © Nova Development, Art Explosion*; James Teason; Lorraine Epstein; Peter Geissler |
| 10-11 | WORLD BOOK illustration |
| 12-13 | Annabel Milne; James Teason |
| 14-15 | Darrell Wiskur; Lorraine Epstein; WORLD BOOK illustration; James Teason; WORLD BOOK illustration; WORLD BOOK illustration; WORLD BOOK illustration |
| 16-17 | Eileen Mueller Neill; Peter Geissler; Eileen Mueller Neill |
| 18-19 | George Suyeoka; Eileen Mueller Neill; Nigel Alexander |
| 20-21 | Peter Geissler; WORLD BOOK illustration; WORLD BOOK illustration; © John Murray, Bruce Coleman Collection*; James Teason |
| 22-23 | James Teason; Yoshi Miyake |
| 24-25 | Angela Lumley; James Teason; James Teason; James Teason |
| 26-27 | © Photri, Robert Harding Picture Library*; © Adrian Davies, Bruce Coleman Collection*; © Fredy Mercay, Bruce Coleman Collection*; Joan Holub |
| 28-29 | Roberta Polfus; Eileen Mueller Neill |
| 30-31 | Eileen Mueller Neill |
| 32-33 | Mike Mogg |
| 34-35 | James Teason; James Teason; James Teason; Peter Geissler; Peter Geissler |
| 36-37 | Eileen Mueller Neill; James Teason; Peter Geissler; Peter Geissler; Peter Geissler |
| 38-39 | Peter Geissler; © David Muench*; George Suyeoka |
| 40-41 | Robert Keys; Jane Pickering; Eileen Mueller Neill |
| 42-43 | Oxford Illustrators, Ltd.; © David Muench* |
| 44-45 | © Alvin E. Staffen, NAS/Photo Researchers*; © Jane Burton, Photo Researchers*; © Joan E. Rahn*; © E. R. Degginger*; © E. R. Degginger*; Peter Geissler; Peter Geissler |
| 46-47 | © Patrick Loertscher, Bruce Coleman Collection*; © M. P. L. Fogden, Bruce Coleman Collection*; © Edward S. Ross*; Edward S. Ross* |
| 48-49 | © E. R. Degginger*; © Jane Burton, Bruce Coleman Collection*; Jane Burton, Bruce Coleman Collection*; Harry McNaught; © Russ Kinne, Photo Researchers* |
| 50-51 | CHILDCRAFT photo; © Prato, Bruce Coleman Collection*; © Bendel, Zefa Picture Library; © Anheuser Busch*; David Webb |
| 52-53 | Peter Geissler; Peter Geissler; Peter Geissler; Tony Gibbons; Lou Bory; © Jan Hinsch, Science Photo Library*; Lou Bory |
| 54-55 | © Les Blacklock, Tom Stack & Associates*; Jane Pickering; Pat Harby; David Webb |